Thomas Turner Wysong

**The rocks of Deer Creek, Harford County**

Their legends and history

Thomas Turner Wysong

**The rocks of Deer Creek, Harford County**
*Their legends and history*

ISBN/EAN: 9783337152260

Printed in Europe, USA, Canada, Australia, Japan

Cover: Foto ©Andreas Hilbeck / pixelio.de

More available books at **www.hansebooks.com**

# THE ROCKS
## OF
# DEER CREEK,

### HARFORD COUNTY, MARYLAND.

### THEIR LEGENDS AND HISTORY.

BY
THOMAS TURNER WYSONG,
OF
"SHIRLEY, NEAR THE ROCKS."

TWO ILLUSTRATIONS.

BALTIMORE:
PRINTED BY A. J. CONLON,
No. 23 SOUTH STREET.
1880

Entered, according to the Act of Congress, in the year 1880,

BY THOMAS TURNER WYSONG,

In the Office of the Librarian of Congress, at Washington, D. C.

TO MY FRIENDS
OF
MARYLAND AND OF THE DISTRICT OF COLUMBIA,
OF PENNSYLVANIA, AND OF VIRGINIA AS
IT WAS TERRITORIALLY AT THE
DATE OF MY BIRTH,
MAY 20, 1817,

*THIS BOOK OF*

Interwoven and Intermingled Fact and Fancy,

Is Affectionately Inscribed by

THE AUTHOR.

# INTRODUCTION.

My residence is about a mile, as the bird flies, from the celebrated Rocks of Deer Creek. I first saw this great natural curiosity in the Spring of 1844. I was then young, and did not dream that my advanced years would be passed almost under its shadows. But He who appoints the bounds of our habitations has so ordered. To-day I occupy the place which I have named, for peculiar reasons, "Shirley, near the Rocks."

Since I have lived in this locality I have been observant of much apparent interest in the Rocks, and have read numerous compositions, both in prose and poetry, descriptive of them. These were generally the essays of the young, inspired by the beauties and sublimities of the scenes around them. Of the objects seen, none have excited more interest than the King and Queen Seats. Who made them?—for what purpose were they used?—have been frequent enquiries. These interrogatories suggested the writing of "The Last King and Queen of the Rocks of Deer Creek." Having done so for the instruction and entertainment of the young people especially, it occurred to me that a series of sketches, mingling fact with fancy, might give them pleasure, and, perhaps, be of some profit to them. These I have written, and they are to be found in this small and unpretentious volume.

I hope that the character of these compositions will give offence to no one, not even the most conscientious. They are, indeed, the interweaving of fact with fancy, but the facts are more numerous than one would imagine who has not studied the locality and its history as I have done. Add to these facts the laws, customs and usages of the original inhabitants of the country, referred to in these stories, and the amount of absolute fiction is not great. My apology for the presence of fiction at all is, that it is, as I use it, a mirror—a reflection of the truth. Nature responds to imagination, and imagination is the handmaid of Nature. Shakespeare is read by all, not because his characters and scenes are not fictitious, but rather because his imaginings mirror the truths of Nature. That sublimest creation of poetic genius, the Book of Job, the Divine inspiration of which is not doubted, is a sacred drama, the persons of which, though they may not have had existence in fact, are nevertheless real, because they are truthful. Paradise Lost and the Pilgrim's Progress are both creations of fancy, but not therefore pernicious. If strict, literal fact is alone to be tolerated, then all books embellished with the colors of imagination must be discarded, though imagination be the medium for the conveyance of truth.

I am the more solicitous that the facts and truthful fancies of this book shall be read, because of the changes that will be wrought by the improvements now in progress and promised in the vicinity of the Rocks. The iron horse will soon be running along our streams and through our valleys, the smoke of the locomotive will curl its wreaths about the summits of the Rocks, partially hiding them from view. The substitution of the realities of the commercial and business life for the poetries of undisturbed Nature is inevitable.

THE AUTHOR.

# INTRODUCTION TO SECOND EDITION.

THE favor with which the first edition of one thousand copies of "THE ROCKS OF DEER CREEK; THEIR LEGENDS AND HISTORY," has been received, encourages the issue of a second edition indefinitely large. The sale of so many copies in so brief a space of time shows that the interest is in the Rocks as a natural curiosity of great attraction; and this fact is a compliment to the intelligence and taste of the many who have purchased and read the book. Of the hundreds who were courteously solicited to patronize this home production, scarce a half-dozen lacked courtesy in their refusal to do so, and charity believes that the majority of this insignificant number were prompted by no unworthy motives. Occasionally there is found in the forests a rare bird, in the waters a rare fish, in the fields a rare beast; why, therefore, should it be thought a strange thing when there is found occasionally among those animals who, as has been scientifically determined, possess the qualities and characteristics of all the inferior animals, one to whom the presentation of a book constitutes a grave offence. Some members of the *genus homo*—the microcosm—never read a book, not because they have no knowledge of letters, but because all letters are offensive to them.

Care has been taken in making up the present edition to avoid as much as possible the defects and blemishes of the first. Both grammatical and typographical errors exist in the former, and fortunate it will be if none shall be found in the latter. The effort to secure perfection of form will be appreciated, and the failure to do so will be forgiven by all generous readers.

This book is larger; other legends have been added; the facts and incidents are more numerous. It is large enough. We launch our boat, which, though not

> "—— as goodly and strong and staunch
> As ever weathered a wintry sea,"

will nevertheless, we hope,

> "—— sail securely, and safely reach
> The Fortunate Isles, on whose shining beach
> The sights we see, and the sounds we hear,
> Will be those of joy, and not of fear."

THE AUTHOR.

# CONTENTS.

|  | PAGE. |
|---|---|
| Title | 1 |
| Dedication | 3 |
| Introduction | 5 |
| Introduction to Second Edition | 9 |
| Description of the Rocks | 13 |
| Razuka; a Legend of Rock Ridge Lake | 15 |
| The Last King and Queen of the Rocks of Deer Creek | 22 |
| The Last Indian of Deer Creek | 28 |
| The Hermit of the Otter Rock | 33 |
| The Robber's Den; or, The Learned Philologist | 41 |
| The Enchantress of Hunting Ridge | 46 |
| The Aged Trapper, Hunter and Fisherman of the Indian Cupboard | 51 |
| The Mine Old Fields; or, The Gathering of the Witches | 58 |
| The Falling Branch; or, The Captured Bride | 64 |
| The Eagle | 71 |
| The Witch Rabbit | 72 |
| The Big Snake | 73 |
| Whitsuntide | 74 |
| The Perilous Feat | 75 |
| An Act of Vandalism | 76 |
| Canal and Railroad | 77 |
| The Original Moonshiner | 79 |
| The Monuments of the Giants | 81 |
| The Field of Darts | 84 |
| The Chrome Pits | 86 |
| The Slate Quarries | 87 |
| The Horse Epidemic and the Guinea-Man's Pony | 89 |
| The Church of the Rocks | 92 |

## CONTENTS.

| | PAGE. |
|---|---|
| Mike's Rock | 94 |
| The Ancient Mill and the Honest Miller | 95 |
| The Oldest Inhabitant | 98 |
| The Youngest Inhabitants | 100 |
| The Original Inhabitants | 101 |
| The Massacre of the Mingoes | 103 |
| Rocks Literature | 105 |
|     Introduction thereto | 106 |
|     Selections therefrom, in Prose and Poetry | 107 |
|         *a.* Description of the Rocks in Prose | 107 |
|         *b.* Stanzas on King and Queen Seats | 107 |
|         *c.* Description of the Rocks in Poetry | 108 |
|         *d.* The Fern | 109 |
|         *e.* The Old Mill | 112 |
| A Prophecy | 116 |
| Mason and Dixon's Line | 122 |
| A Literary Curiosity | 123 |

## ILLUSTRATIONS.

| | |
|---|---|
| The Rocks of Deer Creek | Front of Title. |
| The Falling Branch | Page 64 |

# THE ROCKS OF DEER CREEK.

## DESCRIPTION OF THE ROCKS.

The Rocks of Deer Creek are in Harford County, Maryland, distant nine miles north-east of Bel Air, the county seat, and seven miles south of the boundary line between Maryland and Pennsylvania. The waters of Deer Creek, forcing their way at an indefinite time past through Rock Ridge, have left on either side an immense pile of massive rocks, three hundred and eighty-five feet in height, which, with the plunging waters of the romantic river which runs at their base and the contiguous scenes, constitute a rare picture of sublimity and beauty. The western rocks are more accessible, and of greater attraction to visitors. The view from them is less obstructed and more distant, embracing within its range hill and dale, forest and field, river and brook, farm-house and hamlet. On them are the King and Queen Seats. To the verge of their precipice was driven, by a madman, Bold Hector, that noble horse, which was as deserving of a monument as was Bucephalus, the war horse of Alexander. At their base the Eagle was killed, and also the last wolf and the last deer. These, with other historical incidents, increase the interest felt in the Rocks, the monuments of mighty and mysterious forces exerted in the unknown past.

Every genuine Harfordonian is enthusiastic in his admiration of the Rocks. They are with him the Great Curiosity; they belong to him; he is proud of them. He loves them, because associated with them are memories of happy hours passed with congenial associates on their summits or at their base by the waters of his favorite stream. Their inspirations are sweet to him, and their presence creates sympathies loving and tender. In their presence he has a higher appreciation of Nature, and an intenser sympathy with the spirit of poetry which dwells amid such scenes. Here, as beautifully expressed by our own great poet, whose highest, purest inspirations are due to that " sweet spirit which fills the world;" here, amid everlasting hills, mountain and shattered cliff, and green valley, and river and brook, and the silent majesty of deep woods—

> In many a lazy syllable repeating
> Their old poetic legends to the winds,

his thoughts are uplifted from earth. And such also is the interest he feels in the general library of the Rocks, consisting of many volumes of rare informations.

Will the coming of the Railroad and the development of the commercial and business life, as has been feared, lessen the attractions of the Rocks? The poetries of Nature will still be there, and the presence of the accidents of artificial life may heighten by contrast the interest, making the poetries of Nature more poetical. Happily, the approach by the Railroad, especially from the South, will open up a view of the Rocks surpassing in attractiveness. Passengers from that direction, in crossing the bridge over the Creek at the head of the dam, will have a view of the upper portion of the Rocks, which by a well known quality of the mind will exaggerate the whole picture. Mightier structures they will seem to be, having their foundations in greater depths, because their summits tower upward, touching the heavens. The Rocks, their legends and history, the poetries of Nature made more poetical by the contrasts suggested by the thundering train and smoking locomotive, will ever be sources of interest; and that singular enthusiasm felt by those whose dwelling-places are not distant from the Great Curiosity will abide.

---

# RAZUKA;

### A LEGEND OF ROCK RIDGE LAKE.

---

The Rocks of Deer Creek are the great natural curiosity of Harford County, Md. Who first discovered them? What was their condition at the time of discovery? These questions may not be capable of satisfactory answers. A tradition of the distant and uncertain past is that the first white man who visited that locality did not find it as it now is. Instead of the gorge, and the rocks, and the river running at their base, there was an impact rock ridge, holding against its gigantic breast the waters of a mighty lake, and throwing from its summit, four hundred feet in height, the waters of Deer Creek. The physical features of the ridge, and the characteristics of the low lands for at least five miles above it, justify the conjecture that the traditionary lake and cataract are not myths. In the absence of certain historical information, it may be allowable to accept the tradition as in accordance substantially with the facts. Of the name of the first discoverer we have no available knowledge. If his name is recorded, it may be found in some musty volume of some foreign library. There is a bare possibility that some adventurer, associated with the expedition of the celebrated Captain John Smith, the founder of the colony of Jamestown, Virginia, who in his exploration of the Chesapeake Bay and its tributaries, sailed as far as the mouth of the Susquehanna river, may have heard, on the arrival of the expedition at that locality, of the wonders of the not distant wilderness—scarce a day's journey —and that he was the first civilized man who gazed upon those wonderful exhibitions of nature. It may be that to a Jesuit father, who had penetrated the wilderness in the prosecution of his sacred mission, the honor of discovery is due. These holy fathers were the earliest explorers of our Western territories and inland seas and rivers. They were the spiritual guides and counsellors of many of the North American Indians, and in the furtherance of their work rescued many a wonder of nature from the gloom of the primeval forest. But even though these conjectures be inadmissible, and we should be left to the judgment that at the discovery of this continent by Columbus, in 1492, the Rocks and the Ridge were essentially what they are at the present time, such a conviction does not destroy our faith in the existence of the lake and fall at some more distant period in the past. The testimony of the ridge and valleys assures our belief. We naturally regret that the pent-up waters of Deer Creek exerted so soon that resistless energy which clove asunder a mountain and reduced their volume to the comparatively small stream of to-day. There is beauty in the sinuous Deer Creek, threading its way between abrupt wooded hills and along fertile valleys; also sublimity in the Rocks and rapids as they now are; but how much more of grandeur in the mighty lake and the lofty cataract, rivalling the Falls of Montmorenci or those of the Yosemite Valley.

An ancient bard, whose name is unknown, sang of the Rocks of Deer Creek:

A bare and isolated rock,
On which no tuft of moss has ever grown;
In front a precipice descends far down,
Where a rapid river sweeps along.
Behind, nature has shaped an opening in the cliff
(Which looks with frowning brows upon the scene),
To the resemblance of a lovely garden;
There wild flowers bloom, and scent the evening breeze;
There birds resort and warble all day long;
*There lovers meet and whisper tales of love.*

I have italicized the last line, and for two reasons; first, because it is as true of the present as the past; and second, because it recalls the legend of the Lake and the Rocks, which was learned from the aged and venerable hermit of the Otter Rock.

There once lived on the northern borders of the lake, in the wigwam of her father, a noted chieftain in his day, an Indian maiden of exceeding beauty and rare fascination. This latter statement may be received with incredulity by those who have not had the opportunity of observing the North American Indians in their natural state, removed from the contamination of civilization. The hermit assured me that it is nevertheless true, and I proceed in his own language to describe the attractions of Razuka, the Beauty of the Lake:

"Slender, delicate and elastic as a reed swaying in the currents of a gentle breeze, above the ordinary height, while all the outlines of her graceful figure displayed the lithe and fragile symmetry of girlish years with the mature development of perfect womanhood. Her brow and face were dark, and the rich blood crimsoned her full pouting lips, and flushed peach-like through the golden hue of her cheeks with as warm a tide as ever burned in the impassioned cheeks of an Anglo-Norman beauty. Her long straight hair was of the deepest black. Her eyes had the long almond orbits and long fringed lashes, which are deemed the rarest charms of Italian beauty, and the large soft pupils of the deepest, clearest hazel swam in a field of nacry bluish lustre, which could be compared to nothing but the finest mother-of-pearl. Her teeth were of perfect whiteness, and her features had a harmony and unison entirely their own, a soft, tranquil, half unconcious majesty of stillness."

Such is the very imperfect recollection of the description of the beauty of Razuka, the loveliest of her tribe. Habituated to labor, as all Indian women are, it was but pastime to paddle the light bark canoe, which was her favorite employment. On the lake alone, angling for the fish which abounded in it, she passed many days of her happy life. This life, so free from the anxieties and perplexities of the artificial life of civilized communities, might have been protracted indefinitely but for the possession of the personal attractions that entitled her to the name she bore, Razuka, the Beauty of the Lake. Not only the young men of her own tribe, but those of other and distant tribes, were wont to seek her presence at the wigwam of her father, or gathering on the shores of the lake, gaze with fixed look upon the Beauty shooting her frail canoe with the speed of the arrow through the glassy waters. At one time, having passed entirely over the lake to the opposite shore, she was attracted by the beauty of a wild rose, some distance from the bank, and was about making an effort to secure it, when she heard the rumbling of the not distant thunder. Turning her face to the west, she observed a portentous storm-cloud gathering on the horizon. Anxious, she turned the prow of the boat homeward and rowing with energy, reached the middle of the lake, when the storm fell in its fury upon the waters. Standing upon the shore near the wigwam was a young man of another tribe, who had been smitten by the charms of Razuka, and solicitous for the welfare of her whose life was evidently imperilled, entered hurriedly a canoe lying near by, and pushed out rapidly upon the storm-lashed lake to rescue, if possible, the endangered. Happily he reached her, and taking her into his stronger boat, after almost superhuman exertion, brought her in safety to her home. The rescuer, whose timidity had hitherto deterred him from any marked demonstration of interest in Razuka, now very naturally hoped that the heroic deed he had done would recommend him to the favorable consideration of the chief, the father of the saved; and having awakened the sentiment of gratitude in the mind of the daughter, it might eventually lead to the possession of the prize he coveted. Under ordinary circumstances, such doubtless would have been the case, but unhappily for the cherished hopes of the noble rescuer, Razuka had, unknown to her family, reciprocated the affections of another. Chocorea, the son of a Maquas chief, was the favored one. The father of Razuka, ignorant that the interest of his daughter was endangered, and feeling the obligation of gratitude, would have encouraged the aspirations of the saviour of his idolized child. He intimated to Razuka that possibly her union with the Swan might promote her happiness, and if so, to himself the alliance would not be objectionable. Desirous to undeceive her father, and unwilling that her rescuer should cherish a hope that could not be realized, she frankly declared that her heart belonged to another—to Chocorea, the son of the chief of the Massawomikes, the inveterate foes of her tribe.

"Never," said the chief, her father, "shall the daughter of a Susquehannock wed the son of a Maquas," (the Massawomikes were sometimes so called.) "The Maquas are dogs. These forests had been from time immemorial the undisturbed hunting-grounds of my people, and in this lake they caught at pleasure the white belly and the blue fin, and below the falls, in the water of our river, the shad, the herring and the eel; and my people had hoped that they would sit by their fires unmolested, and smoke their pipes in peace while sun and moon endured; but, alas! in an evil day the prowling wolves of the frozen lakes and haunted forests, the sneaking Maquas, came, and but for the strength of my arm and the arms of my noble braves, many of whom fell by the arrows of the hated ones, my people would have been swept from the earth, as the north wind sweeps the dry leaves from the woodlands. Murderers the Maquas are—robbers, sneaks! No Maquas shall ever wed the daughter of Nieskan, the Susquehannock, and the life of the insolent shall atone for his presumption." This threat was put into execution.

In the twilight of the same evening when these ominous words were uttered, Razuka met Chocorea in the glen (their usual place of meeting), in the rear of her father's wigwam. That interview was hurried and anxious, and resulted in the determination of Razuka to leave the wigwam of her father for the distant home of her hated lover. A meeting was appointed for the ensuing evening to determine the time and mode of their departure. That interview never took place. On the morning of that day, by the hand of the angered father, Chocorea, the lover of Razuka, was slain, and his body was thrown into the lake. The report of a firearm announced the fearful tidings to Razuka, and life for her had no further charms.

Standing, like some grim sentinel, on the southern border of the lake, was a gigantic and precipitous rock, which threw its shadows upon its waters. To the summit of this eminence Razuka, immediately upon the report of the death of Chocorea, made her way, and, fastening to her body a stone of heavy weight, secured by a cord made of the bark of the birch tree, threw herself into the dark waters.

><ul>"On the strand
Two sleeping bodies afterward were found,
Chocorea and Razuka, joined in death
As they had been in life. Their spirits, too,
(So the untutored children of the woods
Believed) had gone to happier grounds—
The Red Man's paradise—to live and love
Forever there."

And furthermore, the legend says that at that lone rock, where Razuka met her fate, is seen at summer eve a great enchantress,

>"Who will sometimes pour
Such glowing tales of love into your ear,
That, in a transport, you will spread your arms,
And clasp a lovely vision."

## THE LAST KING AND QUEEN OF THE ROCKS OF DEER CREEK.

On the right bank of Deer Creek, nearly opposite the present residence of E. S. Rogers, Esq., was, two centuries ago, a village of the Susquehannock Indians. Five miles above, on the same stream, fifty yards from where the mill of James Stansbury, Esq., is located, was another village of the same Indians. Two and one-half miles southeast of the Rocks, on the land now in the occupancy of Bennett Grafton, Esq., was a third village. Each of these villages had its own chief, but, for mutual protection and aid, were confederate, acknowledging the supremacy of the chief whose location was in the vicinity of the Rocks. This chief bore the not uncommon Indian name of Bald Eagle. The chief of the upper village was Great Bear; of the lower, Lone Wolf.

In the autumn of the year Lone Wolf, accompanied by several of his braves, visited the Iroquois, then living in the northern part of what is now the State of New York. While there he became enamoured with an Ojibway maiden, who had been captured by the Iroquois in her infancy; and adopted by their chief, was brought up in his wigwam as his own daughter. The stay of the visitors was protracted until the snow began to whiten the earth and the ice to cover the waters, and Lone Wolf would fain have tarried until the snow and ice were melted again. In the charms of the Fern-Shaken-by-the-Wind, as she had been named by her captors, he had found an attraction stronger than that he felt for his own people in the South country. But failing in his efforts to win the affections of the Fern, he resorted to diplomacy, hoping that time, with assiduity of attention, would soften the maiden's heart, and she would ultimately become his wife. The time of his departure having come, he besought the Iroquois chief to allow his adopted daughter and her brother to accompany him to his distant home, promising to return them safely, and laden with valuable presents, when the trees put forth their leaves again. This request was granted. The Fern and her brother accompanied Lone Wolf to his home. Two moons after their arrival the braves of the three confederate villages were summoned to attend a great council, to be held at the Rocks. At the time appointed Bald Eagle and his wife, as was their custom on such occasions, took their places in the seats on the Rocks known as the King and Queen seats, the braves of the tribe and their confederates sitting upon the ground beneath or leaning against the interspersed trees. At a short distance beyond the circle of the assembled warriors sat the women and children of the tribes and their Iroquois visitors. The Fern and her brother listened attentively to the speeches of the different orators. Nor were they unobserved, the maiden particularly. She could not fail to attract attention, for to perfection of form and great symmetry of features, was added a dignity of manner rarely equaled. Among the braves most attracted by the charms of the Fern was The-Bird-that-Flies-High, eldest son of Bald Eagle, and prospective heir to the supreme chieftainship or kingship, as it was sometimes designated. This young brave, taking advantage of a short recess had by the council, approached the Fern, and offered her as a present a trinket of exceeding brilliancy and apparently of great value, which she graciously accepted. This was observed by Lone Wolf, who, under the influence of an unconcealed jealousy, rushed to the spot where the maiden and her admirer were standing, and seizing the trinket, violently wrenched it from her hands, and throwing it upon the ground, trampled it under his feet. Ordinarily such an act would have been promptly resented, but the Bird had too much regard for the dignity of the occasion, and too much respect for the character and authority of his father, the confederate chief, to notice it by immediate and violent resentment. He quietly withdrew from the presence of the maiden, entertaining, however, the purpose to avenge the insult when the fitting opportunity arrived. That opportunity was not long delayed.

Ten days after the close of the council, there was a gathering of the tribes at the lower village, to participate in the ceremonial connected with the rite of purification, a rite imperative in the case of every male infant of the tribe at its eighth day. From a grove of stately oaks, one of which may be seen at this present time, one hundred yards east of the spot on which now stands the house of Mr. Grafton, a procession moved toward Deer Creek, in the waters of which the child was immersed by the venerable priest of the lower village. The rite performed, the procession returned in the order in which it came. The remaining portion of the day was spent in feasting and dancing, in which the Bird participated with seeming enjoyment and forgetful apparently of his purpose to avenge the insult perpetrated by Lone Wolf. True, however, to the instincts of his race, that purpose was still cherished, and only awaited the opportunity of its accomplishment. When about to leave for his village, he challenged Lone Wolf to a trial of skill with the bow and arrow, to take place at the Rocks early on the morning of the succeeding day, suggesting at the same time the Fern as umpre, whose decision would be respected by all. These propositions were gladly accepted by Lone Wolf, as the trial proposed would afford him an opportunity of displaying his acknowledged skill, and also of enjoying the society of the Fern. On the following day, before the frosts had been melted by the rising sun, the contestants met at the place designated. The contest continued until the shadows fell upon the roots of the trees, when Lone Wolf was declared the victor. The crown of laurel was placed on his brow by the umpire, accompanied by a few words complimentary to the skill of the victor, and seemingly expressive of personal interest. The Bird was excited to madness by the seeming preference of the Fern for Lone Wolf, and remembering the insult, suddenly grasped his rival, and rushing with the speed of lightning to the edge of the precipice, threw him headlong into the abyss below. As he was falling, a few plaintive notes of the death-song were heard, and the voice of Lone Wolf was hushed forever.

The Bird made no effort to escape. Submissive to the immemorial custom and imperative law of his race, he sternly awaited the coming of the avenger, and would certainly have been slain, but for the interposition of the Fern. Drawing from the pocket of a belt which she wore the trinket of two jewels that had not been damaged seriously, she offered them to the sister of Lone Wolf, his only surviving relative, as an atonement for the blood of her brother. The offering was accepted by her, as also by her tribe. That trinket of two jewels was the Ar and Thar, erroneously supposed to have been lost by the ancestors of the present race of Indians in their migration to this continent from the East. It had been preserved in the family of Bald Eagle, and highly valued, as its possession gave prosperity, and conferred princely authority and rule. That the Fern should have parted with such a treasure is understood in the light of the fact that she had cherished an attachment for the Bird, and secretly hoped to become his wife.

Three moons subsequently, at the feast of the coming spring, always observed when the first birds made their appearance, there was another gathering of the tribes at the Rocks, to witness the celebration of the nuptials of the Bird-that-Flies-High and of the Fern-Shaken-by-the-Wind. Following immediately this ceremony was the consummation of a design that Bald Eagle had long entertained. Aged and wearied with the responsibilities and labors pertaining to his position as chief ruler of the confederate tribes, he abdicated his authority, and nominated his son as his successor. His choice was ratified by all the tribes. Conducted by the aged priest of the upper tribe to the seats on the Rocks, the Bird-that-Flies-High and the Fern-Shaken-by-the-Wind were formally declared King and Queen of the confederate tribes.

They were the last King and Queen of the Rocks of Deer Creek. Ere many moons waxed and waned the pale faces came. Driven from their homes and from the graves of their forefathers, the confederate tribes fled to the land of the setting sun, finding their last hours and their graves among strangers in the distant wilderness.

Lone Wolf, whose romantic history and tragic death have been related, was buried on the banks of Deer Creek, about six hundred yards above the present residence of Joshua Rutledge, Esq., and often, during the autumnal nights, in the faint light of the waning moon, is seen at that locality a strange apparition. It is thought to be the spirit of the murdered chieftain mingling with the shadows that fall on the rippling waters.

## THE LAST INDIAN OF DEER CREEK.

Mingo Park is the name of the estate of our well-known and respected fellow-citizen, James Stansbury, Esq. This place is most appropriately named. It is derived from Mingo Hill, an abrupt eminence immediately opposite the residence of that gentleman, at the base of which runs and ripples the waters of the far-famed Deer Creek. The hill itself takes its name from Mingo—one of the Mingoes—whose wigwam was located on the lowlands, an hundred yards or more above the position now occupied by the mill of Mr. Stansbury, and on the left bank of the stream.

The Mingoes have become celebrated in Indian history. They originally occupied a large part of the territory now included in the State of New York. They were known by several names. The English called them the Five Nations, because they constituted a confederacy of that number of distinct nations, increased to six by the accession of the

Tuscaroras of Carolina. The French called them Iroquois; the Dutch, Maquas, and the Virginia Indians gave them the name of Massawomikes. At home they were known by the name of Mingoes. At first their habits had been rather agricultural than warlike, but unhappily for their peace, and the well-being of others of their race, they were attacked by the powerful tribe of the Adirondacks, then occupying the country three hundred miles above Trois-Rivieres in Canada. Necessity drove them to war, and by their prowess and success they earned the proud title of the Romans of the West. Nearly exterminating the Adironacks, and proudly exalting themselves on their overthrow, the Iroquois or Mingoes grew rapidly to be the leading tribe of the North, and finally of the whole continent. But, like many of the mighty nations of the earth, they have yielded to a superior force, and there now remains only an handful to recount mournfully the mighty deeds of their valorous fathers. Another race, with its teeming millions, occupies their hunting-grounds and controls their waters. Their fate is the melancholy recollection of a greatness never to be recovered, and the agonizing anticipation of the utter extinction of their race.

The Mingo whose history we record had, as we have seen, his home among the wild, weird scenes of the Upper Deer Creek. His wigwam at first was one of many, for in the locality designated there was a considerable village of his tribe. The coming of the white man drove them from their homes, and they migrated northward and westward, resting for a time in the forests of Pennsylvania and on the plains of Ohio. Mingo alone remained, occupying his wigwam, with his wife and children, and finding his support in the waters of Deer Creek and in the wooded hills that bordered it. The reason of this seemingly singular procedure is, as will appear, but another illustration of the mysterious nature of man and the power of a sentiment.

The Mingoes of Deer Creek made frequent forays upon the Indians living on the waters of the lower Patapsco, and occasionally extended their incursions into Eastern Maryland and Virginia. In one of their adventures they penetrated the country as far south as the eastern shore of the Chesapeake Bay, opposite the mouth of the Potomac, and attacking suddenly and unexpectedly, surprised and captured a large village, with much booty and some prisoners. Among the captives was Watumpka, the daughter of Wesaco, in his day the most celebrated chieftain of the Wicomicos. Brought by her captors to the Rocks of Deer Creek, which at the period referred to was the general rendezvous of the Mingo warriors of the vicinity, and from which they conducted their warlike expeditions, and to which they returned to make distribution of the common spoils, —happily for Watumpka, in the allotment of the prisoners, she fell to the share of Mingo, who had participated in the expedition. This youthful warrior had seen twenty summers. He had already at that age developed into the noblest type of manhood. Six feet in height, of corresponding weight, straight as the arrow he let go from his bow, of perfect features, rather Roman than Indian, and of dignified mien, he was the admiration of his tribe. Added to these physical attractions was a mind and heart intellectual, sympathetic and loving. The artist would have selected him as his ideal, and the female heart chosen him as its possession forever. Of Watumpka it might have been said, Indian though she was, what the immortal bard said of the gentle Desdemona:

> "A maiden never bold,
> Of spirit so still and quiet that her motion
> Blushed at itself."

And of the attractions of her person what Michael Cassio said of the gentle maiden:

> "Tempests themselves, high seas and howling winds,
> As having sense of beauty, do omit
> Their mortal natures, letting safe go by
> The divine" Watumpka.

Mingo saw and was conquered. His captive was the captor. Watumpka submitting resignedly to the fate of the captured—expatriation from her home—and yielding to the ardent wooing of her lover, consented to become his bride. The celebration of the nuptials was in accordance with the rites of the Mingoes, after which she occupied with her husband his wigwam on the banks of the Upper Deer Creek. There, under the shadows of Mingo Hill, in the quiet and patient performance of the duties of her position as wife and mother, she passed the days of her allotted life. Not indeed without feeling the weight of the shadows that fell upon her heart in the recollection of the happy scenes of childhood and youth, and in the remembrance of the loss of a noble father and the care of a tender mother. These were but occasional experiences. The duties of life and the sense of the affections of him she had chosen generally absorbed her thought.

How long Mingo remained on Deer Creek after the occupancy of the country by the whites is not known. The ancestors of some of the present residents of upper Harford knew him to have been there several years after they had settled in the neighborhood—among them Richard Deaver, the great-grandfather of the present George and Richard Deaver, Seniors. That after a time he followed his tribe westward is conjectured; but if so, not until after the death of Watumpka, his captured bride. By the side of the river, under the shadows of the trees, was laid in deepest grief what was mortal of Watumpka, the child of Wesaco the Wicomico, and the wife of Mingo the Massawomike. And it is not difficult, we think, for the occupants of Mingo Park, as they sit by the blazing fire in the winter nights, to imagine that they hear the voice of Mingo, who long since joined Watumpka in the land of spirits, mingling with the voices of the winds without. It is the voice of the shade of the yet living and loving Mingo, which seeks to commune with the shade of the still living and loving Watumpka.

Honnis, a venerable chief of the Wyandots, said to an acquaintance of the writer of this narrative, that the warriors of his nation were called upon to put each one grain of corn into a wooden tray that would hold more than half a bushel, and that before all had done so the tray was full and running over. The Mingoes were a more numerous and powerful nation, covering a great tract of country, estimated to have been twelve hundred miles in length and seven hundred miles in breadth. Along the Susquehanna and its tributaries, among the forests of Deer Creek and in its valleys, were once many of these people. There remained for a while after their departure a single representative of this once mighty nation. He lingered because his captive wife, the beautiful and loving Watumpka, was alien to his people. They had killed her father, Wesaco, the honored chief of the Wicomicos, and made her a captive in a strange land and among a strange people. Obedient to a mysterious quality of the human mind, she became the wife of a Mingo, participating in his toils and sharing in his sympathies. Him alone she loved, and for him and the children she bore to him she lived—to the Mingoes alien forever,—a sentiment that led her to end her life and find her grave among the pale faces, also the inexorable foes of her race.

## THE HERMIT OF THE OTTER ROCK.

YEARS ago—I will not say how many—there lived in the Valley of Virginia a family of English origin. They had emigrated to America, not to better their worldly condition, but to relieve themselves, if possible, of the shadow of a great trouble which had fallen upon them at their former home. The head of the household was of noble birth—the blood of the —— ran in his veins. Unhappily his temper was irascible, and he lacked ability to control its violence. In a controversy with a fellow-nobleman he yielded to its exactions, and struck a blow that almost instantly proved fatal to his antagonist. Conscious of the insufficiency of the provocation that led to the fatal result, and properly fearing the majesty of that equal justice which is a distinguishing characteristic of English law, he fled his country, and under an assumed name came to America, and found, as he thought, a refuge of safety in the province of New Jersey. Having brought with him abundant means, he purchased an estate in the vicinity of what is now ——, and made preparation for the reception of his family. The large reward that had been offered for his arrest stimulated inquiry, and it was learned that he had fled to America. Detectives were put upon his track, and they were likely to accomplish the arrest of the object of their search. Information of these facts coming to the knowledge of the criminal and fugitive, he suddenly and secretly left the locality in which he had been living, and by concealed travel eventually reached the forests of Virginia. Purchasing from Lord Fairfax, then proprietor of the northern neck of Virginia, a tract of land consisting of two thousand acres, a few miles east of the present site of ——, he again prepared for the reception of his wife and children. Here he was secure, and was in a brief time rejoined by his family. At that distant period of the past there were not, as now, large towns, substantially built, and attractive villages, with communities in town and country possessing all the refinements of highly cultured society. There was not a hamlet; only an occasional cabin, connected by paths or the blazings of the trees, and with rare exceptions, the few, isolated inhabitants were as rude and uncultivated as their surroundings. An exception was the family of noble lineage. The oldest child of that family was a son, and at the time of which we write was a young man twenty-four years of age, of cultivated mind, and of much personal attraction. In heart he was as his mother, a woman of gentle nature and sweetness of disposition. And from her he inherited a love of solitude. Though she was the wife of a nobleman of large wealth, and constrained by her position when at home to mingle much in society, it was always without pleasure, and gladly intermitted. This predisposition to solitude was intensified by the occurrence which led to the removal of the family to America. In its wilds at that day, where solitude reigned almost supreme, Walter —— realized the fullest gratification of the inherited and now cultivated predisposition. He communed with nature and with his own spirit, saddened by the remembrance of a great misfortune.

Calamities come not singly. To that family of stricken ones death came in the character of a mysterious plague, and all save Walter —— fell victims to its relentless power. The solitude that he had coveted and enjoyed, now intensified, became insupportable, and he sought relief from its oppressions. Having heard from a trapper of the wild of northeastern Maryland, with its wondrous lake abounding in fish, of the cataract falling from the summit of a rocky ridge four hundred feet in height, and of the rapid river, in the waters of which the otter and the beaver abounded, and of the forests in which roamed the elk, the bear and the deer, he resolved to make it his home, where, undisturbed by human associations, he might commune alone with nature and the denizens of forest and river ; and forgetting, if such were possible, that crime of a parent which had smitten his heart with an inexpressible anguish, wait patiently and submissively for that event which comes to all. Early on the morning of May — he bade adieu to the forests of Virginia, and, after a fatiguing journey of some days, reached his destination. He had not been deceived by the representations of the trapper. He found lake and cataract, waters abounding in fish and forests in game. About one-half mile east of the Rocks of Deer Creek is a massive rock projecting from a precipitous hill into the water. The rock is cavernous, and was a home of otters ; hence its name, the "Otter Rock." On the hill, one hundred yards above the rock, in a thick growth of laurel, the hermit erected a rude hut of fallen logs. The cabin was well concealed from view by the thicket of undergrowth, and having to and from it a narrow, circuitous path, he deemed himself secure from intrusion. The once "petted child of fortune" took up his abode in this solitary place of the wilderness, trusting in his skill in the use of gun and trap and hook to supply him with the material necessary to sustain his physical life, and hoping to escape the recollections of the great wrong that had poisoned so soon the springs of his earthly felicity.

Solitude, to be advantageous, must be for a season only. Communing with ones self cannot long be protracted. Too long apart from his fellows, man will conjure up a thousand beings to converse with his thoughts ; he will give sentiment and even language to inanimate objects. The wild man will people the solitudes of the wilderness with society, and the untutored man in his solitary watchings and walkings among hills and valleys has his fears aroused by traditions of places haunted by spirits and ghouls. Where human associations break not the monotony of speechless existence, there it always is

"Fast in the wilderness and dream of spirits."

So it became with the hermit. Now he lived in an ideal world. Educated from his youth to believe in spiritual existences, he peopled the solitudes with real though invisible beings, and often in his dreams, as also in his waking reveries, communed with them. The Puckwudjimmenees—those fairy beings whom the Algonquins thought planted the acorns from which the forests of oaks grow—not infrequently to his vision

"—— came fleeting by
In the pale autumnal ray."

In the vicinity of his retreat was a gentle spring of cool, limpid water, which he imagined was haunted by those mysterious little people. There is, perhaps, some apology for the superstition, for an ancient legend tells

" How that old fountain was peopled erst by fairies;
That the spirit of their spells
And flowery rites yet on its margin tarries,
And that upon the summer eve, in the silent air still lingers
The wild, sweet music of a band of fay-like singers."

Such solitude could not be sustained, and the hermit turned to the living instincts around him

4

for relief. In so doing he found pleasure. He found in his communings with the occupants of forest and lake, grove and river, rare and exquisite enjoyments, joys denied him by the presence of civilized life, and not found in the dreamy existence he had been living. The birds entertained him with rarest songs of sweetest melodies, and to his ear the howl of the wolf and the cry of the panther were music. So also the scream of the eagle and the hissing of the serpent. With all the habitants of woods and waters he cultivated intimate relations. He recognized them as friends, and deported himself towards them as such. His friendship was reciprocated, and on their part was confiding. Had he been seen in his wanderings through the woodlands, or in his solitary walkings by the river's side, strange phenomena would have been witnessed. The birds accompanied him, flitting after him from tree to tree, or bush to bush, reluctant, seemingly, to be absent from one whom they manifestly esteemed and loved. The fish recognized his voice, and upon his appearance on the banks of the streams would gather to his presence. They fed from his hand as trustingly as the child feeds from the hands of a loving mother. The raccoon, the opossum, the wildcat and the timid deer were equally confiding. An Adam in his Eden, he ruled the beasts of the field, the birds of the air, and the fishes of the waters. If his physical necessities required the offering of the confiding, that sacrifice was made with the utmost tenderness and consideration.

The hermit was not always indifferent to human associations. Rarely, indeed, did he leave his seclusion to mingle with men. At distant intervals the hermitage was visited by persons prompted by curiosity, if by no other motive. These rare occasions were enjoyed by him, and to his visitors were of great interest. His facility of communication was great, and at the times referred to his conversations were intensive in their character, the logical reaction from the life of seclusion he had led.

Age came to the hermit, and with it thoughts of other days and sweeter joys. Present to his vision often was the image of his mother, and in the slumbers of the night he would dream that he heard her, as in the days of his childhood, breathing blessings upon him. He awoke to find it but an illusive dream. Sickness came, and with it fever, picturing images of terror. The vigils of the night brought with them the sense of loneliness, and the mornings gave no relief. Alone in the wilderness, without the sympathy of his kind, and by infirmity denied the happiness he had derived from association with the instincts around him, he passed the days of his closing life. He was then heard to say he was thinking of his mother—

> "Thy gentle hand seems lightly still caressing
> The flaxen hair so loved, so prized by thee,
> And as in days gone by, I hear thy blessing
> Breathed, oh! so earnestly."

The end came. The solitary watcher by the couch of the departing was a lone star. Looking upward, he gazed long and intently upon it, and interpreted the beautiful phenomenon as prophetic of joys beyond it, where He abides who dwells in the light inaccessible. His last earthly vision was the fading image of his mother.

> "Even thine image now,
> The image of the lovely form, that shone,
> The starlight of my childhood, seems to fade
> From memory's vision. 'Tis as some pale tint
> Upon the twilight wave, a broken glimpse
> Of something beautiful and dearly loved
> In far gone years, a dim and tender dream,
> That, like a faint bow, on a darkened sky,
> Lies on my clouded brain."

Times change, and men and things change with them. The lake and cataract no longer exist. Under the shadows of the Rocks human habitations are built. The waters of Deer Creek are utilized in the production of the necessities and conveniences of civilized and, in a certain sense, artificial life. The rude hut of the hermit has long since disappeared, and the progress of the age threatens greater innovations. But a very brief space of time ago men of singular mien were seen among the hills and along the valleys of Deer Creek, with peculiar instruments in their hands, measuring the surface of the earth as they passed. Unknowingly they stood on the very spot on which rested the Hermit of the Otter Rock, and had they not been so intent on pursuing their curious vocation, they might have heard the voice of a mysterious though invisible stranger bidding them, "Begone!" For have not these men reported that these hills and valleys shall soon reverberate with the loud whistlings of the "locomotive" and the thunderings of the "train?" And such will be the substitution for the poetries of nature in the solitudes of the wilderness.

## THE ROBBER'S DEN; OR, THE LEARNED PHILOLOGIST.

A short distance above the Otter Rock, on the opposite bank of Deer Creek, and in view of the Rocks, is a large cavernous rock, that was, as tradition informs us, in the far past the retreat of an unhappy man, whose hands, like those of Ishmael, the brother of Isaac, the son of Abraham, were against every man, and every man's hand against him. The entrance to the cave is now partially closed by portions of its roof, which have fallen. Directly opposite, and near to the water, was a narrow path, used at first by the Indians in their journeyings to and from the Rocks of Deer Creek and the waters of the Chesapeake Bay and Patapsco River, afterwards by the original white settlers in their travel from one neighborhood to another.

The occupant of the cavern had been reared in affluence and amidst elevating and refining associations. Born in Germany, he received his early education in a gymnasium, an institution answering to an American college. Afterwards he became a student of the University of Heidelberg, one of the largest educational institutions of a land which has ever been distinguished for its ripe scholars and learned philosophers. Immediately after the completion of his scholastic studies, he entered the service of the government as an attaché of an Ambassador to the English Court. Of great acuteness of intellect, well skilled in international law and the art of diplomacy, and ever prompt and faithful in

4*

the discharge of the duties of his position, he won the confidence of his superiors, and was recommended to preferment. Unhappily, at that period of English history, the Court was corrupt; from the monarch down to the humblest servant of the State, profligacy of manners generally prevailed. Truth, honor, integrity, virtue, were words that had no meaning, for the sentiments, principles and actions of which they are the representatives had no existence. Influenced by such examples, his moral force was weakened and his sense of right obscured. The tempter came to him in the guise of a gilded bait—the love of money—that not for its own sake, but for the ability it would give him to gratify his depraved appetites and propensities. The German government has always been characterized by a commendable frugality, not parsimoniousness, but a generous economy. Hence, the salary and perquisites of the attache' sufficed to maintain the dignity of his position, but were not enough for its abuse. The Embassy, having failed on several occasions to receive remittances of money that had been made in the usual manner, employed the services of English detectives, who, after several failures, succeeded in fixing the crime of the abstraction of the funds on the subordinate.

The young man, receiving timely information that suspicion had fallen on him, immediately, in the habit of an English laborer, went on board a Dutch vessel then lying in the Thames, which in a few hours thereafter hoisted sail for America. Arrived at new New York, he deemed it unsafe to remain, and having heard of the wilds of Southern Pennsylvania, journeyed thitherward. And after a fatiguing travel of many days, through forests and swamps, and crossing broad rivers, he reached a locality one-half mile east of the present site of Fawn Grove, York county. He built a rude hut of bark, a few yards above the spring, on the farm now in the occupancy of Thomas H. Wright, Esq., and there tarried for a time, subsisting on the game the forest afforded and the trout caught in the waters of Wild Cat Branch. His stay would probably have been protracted, but ascertaining a few months after his coming that several families of English—supposed to have been members of the Society of Friends—had migrated to his vicinity, he hurriedly left, and directing his steps southward, found himself in a few hours amidst the rugged hills and dense forests in the vicinity of the Rocks of Deer Creek, and believing that here, if anywhere, he would be safe from the pursuit of justice, he chose as the place of his refuge the rock now known as the Robber's Den.

Better thoughts came to the unfortunate, and he resolved to expiate, by penitence and reformation, if such could be, the sin that had made him an outcast and a fugitive in the wilds of America. There was, indeed, no church in the wilderness, at the altars of which he could bow, no clergyman to instruct and comfort, but He against whom he had most sinned, who is not confined to temples built with hands, was there in that "void waste," to witness his tears and hear his cries. Alas! there needed only the presence of the tempter and the occasion of temptation—where are they not?—to call forth again the vicious elements of character that had not been destroyed, only suppressed. At that time Mason and Dixon were running and marking the boundary line between the provinces of Maryland and Pennsylvania, and their party had in the progress of their work reached a point near where the road from Fawn Grove to Fellowship Methodist Episcopal Church crosses Wild Cat Branch. At a spring near by, now on the farm of J. L. Glenn, Esq., they had encamped for a few days to await supplies of provisions from Philadelphia, by way of Joppa, then a seaport town in the province of Maryland. From what is now Forest Hill, there ran northward toward the camp of the surveyors the Indian trail of which I have written, along which the packed mules must pass.

On the morning of what promised to be a bright autumnal day, the robber was awakened from his somewhat protracted slumbers by the cries of the muleteers then approaching. Hastily seizing his gun, he made rapidly for the summit of Rock Ridge, one mile southwest of the Rocks, and secreting himself, awaited the coming of the train. In less than an hour it reached that point of the path, and being in range with his rifle, he fired, killing the leading mule. This so alarmed the drivers that they hastily abandoned the mules, and ran in the direction of their camp. Hiding the spoils in a secure place, the robber left the locality of his Den for a time, to avoid the search that he feared would be made for him. In a few weeks he returned to the cave.

In the Den the once accomplished gentleman and honored scholar and diplomate, but now degraded and dishonored man, passed several years of his life, issuing therefrom, as necessity constrained him, to prey upon the unsuspecting and often unarmed travelers. His many deeds of cruel daring are recorded in the " Book of the Chronicles of the Rocks of Deer Creek," but, sadly for our knowledge, these chronicles are written in a language to which we have no adequate key. There has come down to us the interpretation of a few words of the now obsolete language, which gives us some faint idea of the difficulty of translation by the most skilled philologists, if a translation is possible at all. The words are: Nummatchakodtautamoonkanunuonnash—our lusts; Kummogkodonattootimmooctjongannunnouash—our questions; and Noowomantammoonkauunaunash—our loves. Whether this was the language of the Susquehannocks, who originally occupied the country in the vicinity of the Rocks, or of the Lenopes, who possessed the country eastward and northward, or of the Mingoes, who at one period dominated both of these nations, we have not been advised. It may be an admixture of the three, as it is known that the intermingling of tribes did modify dialects. Nor do we know whether the learned may or may not find in the words resemblance to the family of Semetic languages—the Hebrew, Chaldee, Arabic, Punic, Aramean, Syriac, Ethiopic, Hymyaritic. If such could be shown to be the case, then we might hope for the ultimate translation into English of the " Book of the Chronicles of the Rocks of Deer Creek." Such a result would also establish the theory of the eastern origin of the Indians of North America.

The coming of new settlers made the habitation of the robber and philologist untenantable. He could not expose himself to the certainty of detection. Furthermore, just at that time a paper was found by him in the path opposite the Den; its contents were as follows: "By the King, a proclamation for the more effectual reducing and suppressing of pirates and privateers in America, as well on the sea as on the land in great numbers, committing frequent robberies and piracies, which hath occasioned a great prejudice and obstruction to trade and commerce, and given a great scandal and disturbance to our government in those parts."—*London Gazette.*

Whither he went, we do not know; and the only remembrance of the unhappy man is the "Book of the Chronicles of the Rocks of Deer Creek." Who can translate it?


## THE ENCHANTRESS OF HUNTING RIDGE.

Running parallel with Rock Ridge, one and a-half miles north-northwest of the Rocks of Deer Creek, is Hunting Ridge, and, like the first, is high, rugged, and in places precipitous. Both ridges are covered with trees, generally of large growth, and between them is a narrow valley. The whole scene is of the wildest character, and, singularly, to the inhabitants generally of the county of Harford, is almost as much unknown as are the Highlands of Scotland or the mountains of Switzerland. In the narrow valley, at a time far beyond the memory of living man, there dwelt, as the ancient legend tells us, in a rude hut, built of unhewn logs and covered with clapboards, a family consisting of three persons—an aged man, apparently of fourscore years, intellectual in his appearance and courtly in his manners; a venerable woman, intelligent and dignified of mien; their daughter, a young lady possessing much beauty, affable, and of rare intellectual and social accomplishments. Whence they came none knew, and why they should have left a refined and cultivated community to take up their residence in so isolated and forbidding a locality was a mystery to all. After a time the abode was untenanted, and no one knew whither the former occupants had gone. A few years ago a gentleman visited La Grange, the country-seat of E. S. Rogers, Esq., and hearing the legend, was prompted by curiosity, and the interest he felt in the shadowy past, to visit the unknown scenes. About the middle of the afternoon of a summer day he left the residence of his hospitable friend at La Grange, and walked to the locality of whose physical attractions and mythical story he had heard. The experiences of his visit I will give in his own language, as nearly as my memory will permit me:

"Entranced by the grandeur of the hills and the picturesque loveliness of the vale, I lingered until the twilight of the evening came. Warned by the lateness of the hour, I was about to retrace my steps toward La Grange, when I observed, a short distance from me, a rude hut of logs, which gave signs of occupation. Associating this scene with the legend of the mysterious family, I felt an uncontrollable impulse to visit the rude habitation and its inmates. As I approached the dwelling I heard a female voice of exquisite melodiousness, accompanied by a harp, singing—

"When summer flowers are weaving
  Their perfume wreaths in air,
And the zephyr wings receiving
  The love gifts gently bear;
Then memory's spirit stealing,
  Lifts up the veil she wears,
In all their light revealing
  The loved of other years.

"When summer stars are shining
  In the deep, blue midnight sky,
And their brilliant rays entwining,
  Weave coronals on high;
When the fountain's waves are singing
  In tones night only hears,
Then sweet thoughts waken, bringing
  The loved of other years.

"The flowers around me glowing,
  The midnight stars' pure gleams,
The fountain's ceaseless flowing,
  Recalls life's fondest dreams,
Where all be bright in heaven,
  And tranquil are the spheres,
To thee sweet thoughts are given,
  The loved of other years.

"The interest I had felt was now intensified, and immediately upon the cessation of the voice and harp I rapped at the door. It was heard and answered by a gentle voice, bidding me, 'Come in.' I entered, and finding but a single occupant, a young lady, made as though I would leave the room, when a kind but emphatic, 'Be seated,' constrained me to remain. The young lady in whose presence I was possessed great personal attractions. Her features were regular, he form elastic and graceful, showing that no common blood flowed through her veins. An irrepressible desire seized me to know by what strange mutation of fortune one so gifted should have been impelled to bury herself and all her hopes in this desolate wilderness. I was about to enter into conversation, with the view of eliciting information that might give me a clue to the history of the mysterious being, when I felt myself under the influence of a strange spell. In a few moments I was in a profound slumber. How long I slept I did not know, and when I awoke the scene was wholly changed. I was in a princely mansion. In the room a solitary light was gleaming. The windows were draped with heavy silken curtains. A whisper of leaves and the murmur of a fountain were heard coming from without. Delicate flowers, arranged in vases, were shedding their perfume through the room, and the silver lamp shed a soft and radiant light on every object. The only occupant of the room besides myself was a young lady of medium height, pale of complexion, standing, statue-like, in the middle of the room, with a harp in her hand. She sang:

"Deep hidden in the bosom lies
  A talisman of magic power,
An heirloom borrowed from the skies,
  For man in his first sinless hour,
Inwoven in his secret heart
  By some kind, pitying angel's hand,
Eve, Eden saw him sad depart
  A wandering exile through the land.
This, when all other gifts took wing,
  When of each heavenly gift bereft,
He stood a doomed, deserted thing,
  From the great moral wreck was left—
Was left to light the lurid gloom

That gathered o'er in his fall,
To burst, to brighten, and to bloom
O'er ruined Eden, Eve, Earth—all,—
Awakening joys that ne'er were his
In all their matchless pride and power,
Until all other hopes of bliss
Fled from him. In that angry hour,
When Heaven resumed the gifts it gave,
And drove him forth in his despair
To look upon his future grave,
The self-same hand was ready there
As when it plucked the fruit for him.
She touched the gem his bosom bore,
And though till now its light was dim,
A glory like the Cherubim
It from that magic moment wore.
And ever, 'mid the wrong and wrath
Of life, there beameth far above
The darkness dwelling on his path,
The glory gleam of *woman's love*.

"Again the scene changed. I was in the depths of a dark forest. It was midday, but the light of the sun scarce reached me at the spot where I was standing—the overhanging branches of the heavy-foliaged trees were almost impenetrable to its rays. Of the time when I left the princely mansion and its accomplished inmate I had no recollection, nor how I reached the interior of the forest. I saw no road, not even a path, by which I could have entered it. My situation perplexed me; indeed, alarmed me. For the first time in my life I saw myself surrounded by a network of curious circumstances I could not comprehend. My intellect failed me in the perception of my real condition; so also in the apprehension of the means by which I might be relieved from what seemed to me a hopeless imprisonment in the unknown wilderness. The anxieties of my situation awoke me. I was in the library of my friend at La Grange. Looking at the clock upon the mantel, I found that I had been asleep half an hour. I had been under the influence of a great Enchantress."

## THE AGED TRAPPER, HUNTER AND FISHERMAN OF THE INDIAN CUPBOARD.

The Indian Cupboard is a well-known locality one and a-half miles below the Rocks of Deer Creek and one-fourth mile below the ancient mill now owned by heirs of the late J. Bond Preston, Esq. The Cupboard is a cavern entering a bold and projecting rock whose base is washed by the waters of Deer Creek. Within a few yards of this rock is the home of Alexius, the noted trapper, hunter and fisherman. When Alexius first saw the light of day is not known by the writer of this narrative, nor is it important to the interest of the story that it should be known. I am aware that ordinarily such ignorance might be interpreted as evidence of want of interest in the subject of the story, and perhaps as a lack of appreciation of his deeds. Such a judgment would do essential injustice to the hero, and such he was in the truest and most significant sense of that term. If his deeds do not rival those of the celebrated Baron Munchausen in the quality of exaggeration, or those of the Arabian Nights in romantic significance, they are such as to rank him with the celebrities of the time, and to entitle him to a place on the historic page. The place where the infantile cries of Alexius were first heard is among the wild, weird scenes of Upper Deer Creek, in the vicinity of the Rocks so celebrated in story and in song. The great-grandparents of Alexius were from the Island of Madagascar, in the Indian Ocean. Their migration to the American Continent was a forced one. The negroes of Zululand, South Africa, known as daring and aggressive warriors, and unscrupulous as to the means by which they secured their ends, under pretense of a friendly visit, entered Madagascar with hostile purpose, and attacking their unsuspecting and unprepared army, defeated them, taking many prisoners. These they sold to Portuguese traders, who, in turn, transferred them to English dealers in men. Among these were the ancestors of the subject of my story. They were put on board ship, and, after a somewhat tempestuous voyage of ten months, were landed at Joppa, then a seaport town in the province of Maryland. Happily for them and their descendants, they were purchased upon their arrival in America by a humane and benevolent gentleman then residing in the vicinity of Scott's old fields, now Bel Air, the county-seat of Harford.

Before proceeding further in the relation of my story, I will state, by way of parenthesis, that the people of Madagascar are not negroes. They are copper-colored, have straight black hair, and lack those prominent facial features which belong to the African race proper. They were sometimes enslaved, because it was practicable to do so, and profitable because their better looks made their possession more desirable. Enslaved, they intermarried with the inferior race, and hence but few, if any, remain of unmixed Island blood.

It is due to the character of slaveholders generally of that early period in the history of our Continent, to say that they were not deficient in those qualities that were needed to the discharge of the duties of their relations as masters. Their servants—such they were called—were well fed, well clothed, and their tasks, unlike those of Egyptian bondmen, were not heavy. To them was imparted a measure of education, and their attendance upon religious service was encouraged. In their early years they were allowed the utmost latitude of liberty. Basking in the sun, rolling in the sand, wading in the water, and an occasional siesta, constituted chiefly their summer employment; the winter, in the ashes by the blazing hickory fire, the occasional episode, snow-balling or sliding on the ice. The only fear of the youthful negro was of his irate mamma, whose habit of persistent beatings has often suggested the inquiry, "Is the African woman destitute of sympathy?" Many a negro child has been shielded from the cruel treatment of its mother by the authority of a sympathetic master or mistress. Instincts are hereditary, and though they may be modified by time and circumstances, often survive in their original character, with more or less distinctness, for many generations. The woman in Africa who will barter her child for gain, in America may inflict cruel chastisements. Alexius was fortunate in the possession of his Madagascan mother, she having all that solicitude for her offspring, and exercising that maternal care which insured their comfort; and having in his mistress a lady of great benevolence of character and kindness of heart, his youthful life was happy.

Alexius developed at a very early age those tastes and qualities which have made him so celebrated in the annals of Deer Creek as a most skillful and successful trapper, hunter and fisherman. Retiring in his nature, he loved the solitudes of the forest, and found in communion with its occupants the gratification denied by the common pursuits of life. And it was thus in his association with birds and fishes. At that period the forests of Deer Creek abounded in game, and its waters in fish. In the woods were raccoons, opossums, ground-hogs, wild-cats, and smaller game; in the streams fall-fish, perch, eels, trout and turtle. The favorite game of our hunter was the ground-hog, or wood-chuck, as naturalists call it; and many are the wonderful and marvelous stories told of his adventures with this animal. Like a skillful hunter as he was, his first effort was to secure their confidence. He frequented their burrows and made their acquaintance. He had the peculiar faculty of making himself understood by them. This animal is not alone in its susceptibility to education. The flea has been trained to know the voice of its master, and to be obedient to his commands. Unhappily for the confiding chuck, the motive of the seemingly friendly hunter was sinister; he smiled only to betray, and the confidence of the simple chuck was his destruction. 'Possum-hunting was an exciting pastime. In the woods of Rock Ridge and contiguous hills he passed much time in this, to him, pleasing pursuit. His habit was to leave his retreat about nightfall, taking with him his two trusty dogs, Bell and Traveler. Once on a trail, they followed it unerringly to the hiding-places of the game, which were usually in the thick boughs of some lofty tree, or in the rocky caves with which the ridges abound. The coon treed, the hunter ascended the tree with almost the agility of the squirrel, and, ascertaining the position of the game, proceeded to dislodge it. This he did either by a violent shaking of the limb, or by pushing the animal from his perch with a long and heavy pole. The coon on the ground was immediately secured by the dogs. More than once the hunter narrowly escaped the loss of his life in these perilous adventures, and he bears to this day on his hand the mark of the bite of an enraged coon struggling for his liberty. Want of space forbids the enumeration of the many thrilling adventures connected with his pursuit of game in the forests. In the water he was equally successful. Eels of enormous length and size were trophies of the fisherman's skill, as also turtles of great bulk and wonderful strength. Notwithstanding the asseveration of the fisherman, whose veracity it is not our province to question, it is hard to believe that "Big Turtle" supported the weight of a man of one hundred and sixty pounds, and carried him on his back the distance of a half-mile. The theory of Darwin—the survival of the fittest—would lead us to look for animals of larger size at the present than in the past, and there is the remotest possibility that this trophy of our fisherman's skill was one—the last survivor possibly—of a family that had, by a fortuitous and fortunate concurrence of circumstances, been preserved from the power of all trappers, hunters and fishermen, from Nimrod down to the last of his class on Deer Creek.

Our hunter was characterized by an even courage that made him equal to emergencies generally. He was never known to exhibit fear in contest with bird or beast or fish. It was different as to a gigantic snake, a habitue of the hill opposite the old mill above the Cupboard. This snake "was twenty feet long and thick as a man's body." It is conjectured that it was of foreign origin, or was of the Hall's-spring species that in very late times so excited the people of that section of Baltimore county, Md. But whatever may be the opinion of the present generation as to these accounts of the size of the fauna of the past, it is true that our hero was remarkably successful in his favorite vocations. And now, in his old age, he is envied by the younger generation of hunters, trappers and fishermen. He may be seen occasionally bearing homeward, as a trophy of his skill, a fat "chuck," and often in the early spring or summer morning drawing from the waters of Deer Creek the largest fall-fish or the longest eel. The "coon" and the "'possum" are now secure in their retreats, for age has incapacitated him for those exertions necessary to their successful pursuit.

A new day has dawned. An intensive civilization, eager for great achievements, has decreed that the hills and dales of Upper Deer Creek shall no longer rest in their comparative solitudes. The tramroad and the steam engine, with their enormous capacity of transportation, are about to substitute the common modes of travel and trade. The change will bring an increased population, and insure the erection of factories and mills. The theatres of the solitary wanderings and walkings and skillful achievements of our hunter, trapper and fisherman will re-echo with the whirr of the wheel and the sound of the hammer. A new generation, with its real and artificial wants, will take the place of the old, content in its enjoyment of the common modes of life.

The Indian Cupboard, no longer tenantable, has been abandoned. A common country road has marred its beauties, and soon the mighty and mysterious dynamite will reduce its proportions still more. Reluctant to leave a spot endeared to him by so many recollections of the past, the subject of our narrative is building of stone and wood, under the shadow of the Copper Rock, a habitation conformable to the style of modern times, where, as a partial compensation for the great loss he has sustained, the exclusion of the employments and pleasures of the past, he will view the mysterious stranger as it passes by, laden with the productions of the earth and the fruits of human skill.

The story I have told is not of one reared in affluence, a child of fortune, but of a poor man, who has illustrated the dignity of manhood in the faithful discharge of the duties of life as he understood them. And there are those who have owed to him the preservation of their lives from a watery grave in the sometimes excessively swollen and turbulent waters of Deer Creek; and many more for assistances and courtesies that ought not to be forgotten. To that class of the community who worship only the great we have no apology to offer for this remembrance of the humble. We find in such recollection an illustration of the well-known adage, "Act well your part; there all the honor lies."

## THE MINE OLD FIELDS; OR, THE GATHERING OF THE WITCHES.

Two miles east northeast of the Rocks are the Mine Old Fields. This locality, though the Arabia Petrea of this section of Harford County, is not without a certain degree of interest, and may be catalogued with the many curious and attractive natural objects of the neighborhood of the Rocks. It is an elevated plateau of considerable area, abounding in iron ore, chrome and other minerals. Much of the rock is soapstone of a superior quality. From this stone the Susquehannocks and other Indians of the vicinity made their culinary vessels. Occasionally there is found a pot or other relic which is treasured as a souvenir of the distant past. These Fields, as they are called, have never produced wheat, or corn, or other cereals, but did for a time yield an abundant harvest of iron ore, which, being smelted, was manufactured into various articles that the necessities of civilized life demand, and they will, doubtless, upon the completion of the Railroad, yield again their valuable treasures.

A tradition exists that on this territory was found, many years ago, a rich mine of lead; that it was known to the first Mr. Rigdon, settled near by on land now in the occupancy of some of his decendants. He was, in his day, a great hunter, and obtained there, it is said, all the lead he used. There is a similar tradition that in the immediate vicinity of the Rocks there is a gold mine, known to the Susquehannocks, the original inhabitants, the knowledge of which was communicated by them to some white man who visited the locality at an early day. The contractor who made his way by powder, and crowbar and pick through the formidable rock, in the hill immediately beyond the creek, above the mill, found in the rock a substance bearing so strong a resemblance to gold that he conveyed a large specimen to the shanty. There it was for a time to be examined by the curious. But like the discoverers of gold at the settlement of Jamestown, Virginia, expectants were doomed to disappointment. The Mine Old Fields do have iron and chrome, and perhaps lead.

Like other portions of this far-famed section of Harford, the Mine Old Fields have a mythical history. The story of the gathering there by moonlight of the witches to practice their mysterious rites, has come down to us of the present generation. We shall relate it substantially as it was told to an aged citizen by that venerable hermit, whose romantic and touching history is written in this book. That the story may be properly appreciated, it will be necessary to preface it by some preliminary statements.

Many persons believe not only in the power of the devil to assume a corporeal form, but also in his capacity of acting injuriously upon mankind through the instrumentality of others. Baxter, the author of the "Saint's Rest," shared this opinion with many of the wisest and best of England in an age of culture and refinement. The same credulous tone of mind existed in New England in its early history. It is true that at that period belief in witchcraft and other diabolical agencies were popular delusions which were rapidly disappearing from the world, but such men as Cotton Mather and the intelligent inhabitants of Salem were always ready to sustain their belief in such superstitions both from holy writ and philosophy. It was an excess of the imagination, affecting not only the stupid and the dull, but also the highest wrought minds. The early residents of our vicinage were a simple and enthusiastic people, primitive in their manners, and were doubtless affected by the sentiments of their more pretentious fellow citizens northeast of them. The Puritan, then as now, despite the prejudice and repugnancy felt toward him, singularly impressed his views and opinions upon others. In the existence of witches and other malevolent beings and their power of harm, many of our ancestors had the most implicit faith. They saw spirits and witches; to them devils appeared; strange sights were seen, strange sounds were heard. The Jack o' the Lantern was recognized as a personality whose every purpose was evil, and whose following certainly brought perplexity, and even peril of life. The Fay, though extremely diminutive in size, was greatly feared, not so much on account of its physical ability to do harm as of a supposed moral power of evil. The potent words were spell, charm, witchcraft.

Why witches practice incantation on moonlight nights may possibly be explained on philosophical principles. There is no peculiarity, that we are aware of, in the visual organs of a witch. The singular construction of the eye of an owl or an Albinos adapts their sight to moonlight. The retinas of witches are suited to the light of day. 'Tis not that; 'tis this, perhaps. The moon is idiosyncratic; psychologically, she is peculiar, and by the well-known law of sympathy impresses her own nature upon the nature of man. It must be so, or else the word lunacy would not have found a place in our lexicography. Other reasons why the witches were wont to assemble in the Mine Old Fields on moonlight nights are apparent. They had light. Besides, the fears of the people, heightened by moonlight, were a defence to them as strong as the walls of a fortified city. The witches were there, and there they practiced their dark rites. Around the blazing fire and the boiling caldron they, with joined hands, walked during the hours of moonlight—"black spirits and white, red spirits and gray,"—singing:

"Mingle, mingle, mingle,
You that mingle may,"

and invoking the spirits of power, ceased their orgies only when there came to them the gifts of power, in the exercise of which they satanically delighted. The demonstration of the fact that they who gathered in the Mine Old Fields by moonlight were witches, was that people in the vicinity became sick in all sorts of ways, falling into strange fits, crawling under beds and into cupboards, barking like dogs, mewing like cats, bleating like sheep, and lowing like cattle. The doctors were sent for, and they declared that their patients were bewitched. All were superstitious. All believed in diabolical agency. Terror and consternation were in every heart.

Living at that day on Deer Creek, one mile east of the Mine Old Fields, in an humble dwelling, was an aged woman, whose only misfortune—if such it were—was that she was poor and infirm. The other occupants of the hut were an aged Indian woman, one of the very few who remained after her people had migrated westward, and a young man of the class of the "innocents," as the Swiss mountaineers benevolently name such unfortunates as are not endowed at birth with the *sana mens*. Albert, as he was always tenderly called by his aged mother, willingly labored to provide sustenance for the household, and the Indian woman, Maggy, having been taught the art of weaving, contributed also by her industry and skill to the support of the family. Of the aged matron of the lowly household it might have been said, "She that is a widow indeed, and desolate, trusting in God, and continueth in supplication night and day;" and of her assistant, "She hath done what she could." An Eden it was. But the cruelties of suspicion were soon to be felt by the hitherto unsuspecting and confiding household. Trouble came from an unexpected source.

Father G., a prominent man of the neighborhood, in conversation had said, "There have been wizards and witches in all times," and that pious and learned man, Cotton Mather, says, "That if all the spectral appearances and molestations of evil angels, and tricks of necromancy, and bodily apparitions of Satan and his imps, could be collected and counted, that are daily and nightly going on, all righteous and goodly men's hair would stand on ends with horror." "In these parts," continued Father G., "are infernal doings," and pointing significantly toward the cabin which the unsuspecting were abiding in peace, ominously said, "Satan may now abide there." That was sufficient to create in all minds a suspicion that very soon ripened into a conviction, that the aged and decrepit occupant of the cottage, as, perhaps, also her faithful assistant, dealt with familiar spirits, and that much, if not all, the strange evils which afflicted the community were to be attributed to their machinations.

On the morning of the following day the former habitation of the widow was but a pile of smoking ashes. The people said, "The wretches who made a compact with Satan, and inflicted the evils we suffer, have perished. Give God the glory."

From the Mine Old Fields the witches have departed. Their unhallowed rites have ceased; the innocent are at rest. And Father G. has, we hope, expiated his great wrong in the light of a knowledge free from cruel suspicion.

## THE FALLING BRANCH; OR, THE CAPTURED BRIDE.

EMPTYING into Deer Creek, three miles above the Rocks, is Falling Branch. It is so called from the fact that a mile or more above its mouth its waters fall from a rock twenty-five or thirty feet in height, forming a miniature Niagara, which, with the picturesque and romantic surroundings, constitute a most pleasing attraction. To some this curiosity is more attractive than the Rocks, nature not displaying herself in such bold and massive forms, but exceeding in picturesque beauty. It is a wild scene, primitive almost as when the wild man speared the speckled trout that abounded in its waters, or shot the swift deer that frequented the adjacent forests. Here the attention of the visitor is also curiously drawn to a series of stone steps that lead from the base of the rock over which the waters fall to its summit. These steps were seemingly cut by the hand of man. If so, by whom and by what instruments? The Susquehannocks, who dwelt by the locality when discovered by the white man, were men of large size and of much strength, but could physical strength so handle the stone axe or hatchet as to make the achievement possible? If human ingenuity and labor constructed the steps, it may have been done by that previous race whose instruments of labor were of copper or iron, or by the present race, to whom invention has supplied such instruments in their more perfect forms.

Within fifteen or twenty yards of the falls and

directly opposite them are the remains of a mill and a dwelling-house, the former abode of the miller. Why the immediate contiguity of those buildings to the falls? Was the builder and occupier a man of romantic turn of mind? Appreciating the scene, and charmed by the music of the falling waters, were these the motives that prompted him to fix his residence in this wild spot? It would be pleasant to think so, but sadly for our imaginings, the suspicion of utility and economy is suggested. His nearness to the falls obviated the necessity of building a dam of perishable material, or the digging of a race, or the construction of a trunk more than a few feet in length. Wise, worldly wise, was Isaac Jones in his day and generation. But for aught we know, in the heart of that plain man who patiently watched the hopper in the years long gone, when northern Harford was a comparative wilderness, and the progenitors of the pretentious race of the present were a plain folk without ambition to be great, there may have been the highest and the subtliest appreciation of nature in her sublime and beautiful moods, and a susceptibility to art that brought to him the knowledge of that mysterious law—a law operative in the realms of spirit and matter equally, —which harmonizes the creations of the made with the works of the Maker. The artist-born builds not a high house in a *diminutive* and contracted valley, nor a low one on a high hill overlooking an extended plain. These are but few of the many fitnesses of things perceived by the man whom God has created great in his appreciation of the harmonies of nature. Almost a demonstration of the possession of this quality is the row of Lombardy poplars, now in decay, that were planted in front of the dwelling, which, with the native forest trees and rocks and cataract and rapid river, constituted a scene of surpassing attractiveness.

The Falling Branch owes its chief attraction to the story of the Captured Bride, which, though confessedly legendary and mythical, is not without a certain degree of interest, especially to persons of much romantic susceptibility. Arlotto was the only daughter of a gentleman of fortune, whose home was in the vicinity of Hull, England. The attractions of her person and the fascination of her manners, added to a superior mental and moral culture, brought to her presence many admirers. Among them was an officer of the English Army. Young, handsome, accomplished, brave, the scion of a noble family, in all respects worthy of her whose qualities of mind and heart had so strongly attracted him, his suit was encouraged, and after a proper interval of time, they were wedded. The church, or rather cathedral, in which the nuptials were celebrated, was

"A dim and mighty Minster of old times!
A temple shadowy with remembrance
Of the majestic past."

Everything about it told of a race

"—— that nobly, fearlessly,
In their heart's worship poured forth a wealth of love."

There, under its fretted roof, and in the midst of its wrought coronals of ivy, and vine, and leaves, and sculptured rose—"the tenderest image of mortality"—the light which streamed through arch and aisle in harmony with all; that dim, religious light, which is a reminder of the past—of the dim, the shadowy, the heroic past—there, in the select assembly of the high-born, they pledged each to other their troth, and were by the aged and venerable priest pronounced man and wife. Retiring from the church, they were followed by the aged minister and his assistants, singing a recessional hymn, accompanied by the organ, the flood of its harmony bearing up on its high waves their voices attuned to the praise of God. Such was the marriage scene.

The past is always suggestive of the future. The memories of the past, like dim processions of a dream, are associated with visions of the future, though indistinct as dreams that "sink in twilight depths away." Arlotto passed from the altar happy, indeed, in the sense of the love of her now adored husband, but not without thoughts tinged with sadness. Apprehension of coming sorrows was the shadow that fell upon her pathway so soon. "Coming events"—sorrowful and pleasant alike—"cast their shadows before." A few days after the marriage the young officer was ordered to rejoin his regiment, then at Portsmouth, about to embark for America. This summons was the interpretation, in part, of the mysterious revelations that mingled with her present joys fears of future evils.

> "Even so the dark and bright will kiss;
> The sunniest things throw brightest shade,
> And there is even a happiness
> That makes the heart afraid."

The New World was at this period a theatre for

the struggles of giants. France and England were contending for the mastery, and the stake was a continent, with all its possibilities of wealth and power. So desperate was the conflict, and of such magnitude was the issue, that each party was obliged to avail itself of all its resources. To the place of battle, so full of peril to the participants, the youthful officer would have gone alone. He was unwilling that his bride should be subjected to the privations incident to warfare, and to the perils always attending it, greater in this case because of the character of the foe. The savages were generally the allies of the French. Yielding to her entreaties, he consented that she should accompany him.

Arriving in America, the regiment to which the officer belonged was detached to form a part of the army then being raised by the governors of Massachusetts and Connecticut, and designed to operate against the French and Indians, who in large force were threatening the borders of their respective provinces. In a battle fought soon after his entrance upon the campaign, the young officer was wounded, and left upon the field as dead. Arlotto, immediately upon the cessation of the conflict, made her way to the ensanguined field, and after a patient and anxious search found her yet living husband. The dying sufficiently recovered to recognize her whose presence was the only earthly solace left to him. A few words, with difficulty uttered, were expressive of the tenderness and strength of his affection. Arlotto hoped. How delusive that hope!

"A moment more and she
 Knew the fullness of her woe at last!

> One shriek the forests heard—and mute she lay
> And cold; yet clasping still the precious clay
> To her scarce heaving breast."

Awaking from what was less than death and more than sleep, Arlotto became conscious of the presence of a dusky form bending with seeming sympathy over her prostrate body. It was an aged Indian warrior, who, taking her tenderly by the hand, bade her arise, and by further signs indicated his desire that she should follow him. Toward the setting sun they journeyed slowly for some days; then south-eastward until they reached the immediate vicinity of the Falling Branch. There was the home of her captor, a lone cabin in the woods, within hearing of the plunging waters of the cataract. The Indian woman in whose care she was placed, seemingly won by "a form so desolately fair," or touched by the remembrance of some deep sorrow, manifested an unwonted interest in the captive, and cared for her with all the tenderness and solicitude of a mother. The aged warrior and his wife had seen a daughter go to the land of spirits,

> "And ever from that time her fading mien
> And voice, like winds of summer, soft and low,
> Had haunted their dim years."

And fancying that they saw in their captive a resemblance to their only child, whose early death had thrown upon their pathway heavy shadows, their hearts, "with all their wealth of love," were touched by the sorrows of her to whom was left only the memories of the past. In the forest was no temple erected by human hands dedicated to the Sufferer of Calvary. It was a void waste, in which the sound of the church-going bell was not heard; nor priest nor altar was there. Yet in the silent majesty of the deep woods, and in the presence of the silver brook which pours from its full laver the white cascade, was more than the spirit of poetry which dwells amid such scenes. The spirit of the Holy One was there, and valley and brook, and cascade and deep woods and everlasting hills, and the green trees, were a grand minster at the altars of which the devout could worship and the sorrowing find relief. To this temple and to these altars in the green wood, by the side of babbling streams, in the sunlight and the stars' bright gleams, the sufferer went, and thither she led her captors, and there she taught them to listen to the voice of Him whose presence is the glory of all temples and of all altars.

The harp-string too strongly tensioned breaks. Worn with grief and hopeless of relief, Arlotto wasted, and when autumn's last sigh was heard, and the winter's blast, in the first days of spring; when "sound and odors with the breezes play whispering of spring-time," bore to her couch life's farewell sweetness, then she was passing away to that solemnly beautiful sleep, that deep stillness which falls on the silent face of the dead.

Arlotto's life work was ended; its great purposes accomplished. In the depths of the forest, within hearing of the murmuring waters of the Falling Branch, in God's acre she sleeps, and by her side her foster father and mother. In *God's acre* they rest, and

"Into its furrows shall we all be cast,
　In the sure faith that we shall rise again
At the great harvest, when the archangel's blast
　Shall winnow, like a fan, the chaff and grain.

"Then shall the good stand in immortal bloom,
In the fair gardens of that second birth;
And each bright blossom mingle its perfume
With that of flowers which never bloomed on earth."

## THE EAGLE.

"He clasps the crags with hooked hands;
Close to the sun in lonely lands,
Ringed with the azure world he stands,
The wrinkled sea beneath him crawls;
He watches from his mountain walls,
And like a thunderbolt he falls."

Some yards above the Saloon at the Rocks and under the hill, there lived in a small cabin a man by the name of Cully, the father of Arch Cully, so well known in his day by the residents of Rock Ridge and its vicinity. At that early period the Rocks and their surroundings were in almost their original wildness, unaffected by the arts and appliances of civilized life. The axe of the woodman might have been heard now and then, but no house other than the cabin had been erected, and no forge or furnace to mar the scene.

It was wash-day to the aged matron of the hut, and while engaged in the necessary vocation, she heard the cries of the chickens and the excited barkings of the dog without. An eagle, whose nest, with young, was on the summit of the opposite

Rock, had swooped down from her eyrie, and seized with its talons one of the chickens. The little dog, true to its instincts, hastened to the rescue, and chicken, and dog, and eagle were soon engaged in earnest contest. The eagle was likely to succeed in her purpose, when the old lady, grasping her beetle, ran to the rescue, and striking the eagle a deadly blow, carried it in triumph to the cottage.

The eagles, like the original human inhabitants, pressed by the presence of civilized man, have sought their eyries on more distant and secluded heights. Occasionally one may be seen hovering about the summits of the Rocks, as if curious to observe the past homes of its progenitors.

## THE WITCH RABBIT.

AMONG the hills in the vicinity of the Rocks was many years ago a remarkable rabbit. Tradit on tells us that it was of the size of a Jack Rabbit, that well-known habitant of the West, though not of the same species. The hunters of those early times sought by trap and snare to secure it, but without success. Many a charge from musket and shot-gun and rifle was directed toward it fruitlessly. The opinion of our simple fathers was, that the body of that rabbit was the habitation of a witch, and in solemn conference they resolved that it could be slain by a silver bullet only. The scarcity of the precious metal prevented the making of the problematical experiment, and hence the possessed animal was left to wander at will. For many years it has not been seen. The witch may have taken another habitation, or assumed another form. The enlightenment of the community has thrown doubt upon the story, once so implicitly believed. People now-a-days suspect much of the past to be mythical, as it doubtless is, but subjecting everything to a mathematical test, they may forget, as my credulous friend suggests, that there are more things in heaven and earth than are dreamed of in their philosophy. Candor compels us to say that in our philosophy there are no witches save those bewitching ones whose manners captivate the susceptible youths of the stronger sex.

## THE BIG SNAKE.

The existence of a species of snakes of large size in the neighborhood of the Rocks has been reported for many years. Mr. William Jeffrey, an aged citizen of Bel Air, informed us that the track of a snake "broad as a cart wheel" was pointed out to him by his father seventy years ago; that thirty, and again fifty, years thereafter, the serpent itself was seen. The Ancient Trapper avers that in his youth he learned from a reliable source of a snake of extraordinary size, whose home was in the hill opposite the Ancient Mill. By the incredulous, the story was considered doubtful, or supposed to be an exaggeration, but very recently several persons whose truthfulness is not questioned, have declared that they saw the monstrous reptile. The visitor to the Rocks need have no fear, as the animal is most likely to shun the presence of man. And it is probable that the blasting of rocks in the making of the Railroad will induce his majesty to seek another domain in which to enjoy his hitherto acknowledged supremacy over the beasts that crawl.

## WHITSUNTIDE.

For many years the Rocks were a resort at Whitsuntide. The best people of the country patronized the festival. It was a favorable time for making acquaintance and cementing friendships. And I suppose that then, as now, on festal days, Cupid was present, armed *cap-a-pie*, and that his arrows failed not of many a worthy mark. An estimable lady, who died a few years ago, living to be nearly one hundred years of age, was wont to speak with great interest of her visit to the Rocks of Deer Creek at Whitsuntide, when she was a little girl. Her memory of the delicate and refined attentions of Colonel John Streett, a prominent gentleman of Harford county, in those early days, was very distinct, and she failed not to speak of them enthusiastically

The Rocks in later years became at this season a scene of dissipation and rowdyism, and the patronage of the more respectable classes was discontinued. In the procession of years, another change has come. Now, at all seasons, the Rocks are a point of attraction to all classes. The pic-nic, harvest homes, political gatherings, railroad meetings, have substituted Whitsuntide; and upon the completion of the Baltimore and Delta Railroad, the Rocks must, from the attractions of scenery and the salubrity of the air, become the resort of persons from all sections of the county and more distant points.


## THE PERILOUS FEAT.

To say fool-hardy, would be an appropriate addition to qualify the act. A well-known resident of the neighborhood of the Rocks illustrated the truth of the old adage, "When wine is in wit is out," by forcing his horse to the very verge of the precipice, with seeming intention of throwing himself and his noble animal into the fearful abyss below. The sober horse, with more discretion than his drunken master, seeing the peril, turned at the moment of immediate danger, and thus saved himself and rider from certain death. This unhappy man afterward, in an attempt to force his horse across Deer Creek when swollen, was drowned. The particular point on the Creek where he entered the water is said to have been about the head of the dam of Preston's Mills. Thus died ignominiously a man who, but for indulgence in the use of an unnecessary beverage, might have lived for many years, a comfort to his family and an ornament to society. The horse, Bold Hector, as he was not inappropriately named, survived his unfortunate master several years.

## AN ACT OF VANDALISM.

On the summit of the western Rocks was an immense boulder, weighing many tons, poised on a fixed rock so slightly and delicately that a strong man could move it at will, and yet it was so related to the rock upon which it rested, that it required the force of four men, aided by levers, to throw it from its position. These persons, without appreciation of nature, and of mere wantonness, or conceiving the purpose of giving immortality to their names, threw this object of great interest from its position to the rocks below, where it now lies without hope of its ever being replaced in its original location. I have understood that the then proprietor of the Rocks offered a reward for the discovery of the perpetrators of the ignoble deed, but that it was not effectual in securing that end. This may have been fortunate. Otherwise the names of the guilty parties might have been coupled in history with the destroyers of Rome and the burners of the Alexandrian Library.

## CANAL AND RAILROAD.

When the Tide-Water Canal was completed, our citizens agitated the subject of slack-water navigation from a point five miles above La Grange to the mouth of Deer Creek, the accomplishment of which would have made a direct and cheap outlet for our trade to Baltimore and Philadelphia. The idea was born of a felt necessity, but could not have been made practical. Such a project would not have paid. And it has been well for the health of the country bordering Deer Creek that it was impossible of realization. Canals and fevers are synonymous terms.

Instead of slack-water, locks and dams, with increased disease, we shall have a Railroad, and more direct communication with Baltimore, our chief commercial city. Under the direction of a most energetic President and an enterprising Board of

Directors, sustained by citizens along the line, who are awake to its advantages, it is being pushed with commendable vigor, and will, we cannot doubt, be completed in good time.

To our immediate Rocks of Deer Creek neighborhood the effect of the road will be very significant. Our rocks and minerals will be marketable, and the attractions of our scenery will draw many curious visitors. And it is to be hoped that the possessors of the soil will awake from their more than Rip Van Winkle sleep. It is strange that they have slept so long, seeing that around them there are so many examples worthy of imitation. The enterprise, thrift and judgment of the many successful farmers above, and the no less competent tillers of the soil below, should stimulate us to an exertion that may make this comparative wilderness blossom as the rose. The Railroad, completed, will ensure the development of all our interests. Our fields will yield abundant harvests, the waters of Deer Creek will be utilized in the operation of mills, and factories, and furnaces. Our lofty summits will be crowned with the residences of their proprietors, or occupied as the retreats of the wealthy inhabitants of the city.

## THE ORIGINAL MOONSHINER.

Southeast of the Rocks three-fourths of a mile, through a ravine hidden by wooded hills, runs a small stream, having its sources in several springs a short distance above, which gives evidence of occupation and use. Remains of a dam still exist, as also traces of a ditch, leading to what has the appearance of the foundation of a building. For what purpose was the dam built, the ditch dug, and the building erected? The oldest inhabitants cannot answer these interrogatories, and have no tradition in relation thereto. We are therefore left to conjecture the purpose for which they were made. It may have been the location of the distillery of some moonshiner—one of the progenitors of the gentlemen of West Virginia, Tennessee, North Carolina, and elsewhere, who are engaged in illicit distillation, to the great detriment of the revenues of the United States of America. If so, he could not have selected a place more favorable to his vocation.

Since writing the above I have had conversations with James Wann, Esq., and with David Tucker, Sr., an aged citizen, from whom I have learned some facts that may throw doubt on the moonshine theory. They informed me that in the earlier days of Harford the tub-mill was in use, requiring but little water; that the turning of chair-stuff by water, of which little volume was required, was common; as also the distillation of brandies from fruits, requiring comparatively little water. The waters of my brook may have been used for one of these purposes. A remark made by our venerable citizen, Mr. Tucker, throws doubt upon all these speculations. He said that it is not rare to find in the forests of this portion of Harford traces of ditches, sometimes of considerable length, leading to lowlands, and suggested that they might have been used for purposes of irrigation. If so, by whom? Not one of the oldest inhabitants has any knowledge of such use, and none know by whom they were excavated; nor is there tradition bearing upon the subject. Can it be that the people who preceded the Indians in the occupancy of this country, and who have left traces of a superior civilization—the mound-builders or some other race—were the diggers of these ditches, and used them, as suggested, for irrigating uses? Or might they not have been rude aqueducts conveying water to their villages or fortified camps, or, at a later period, to the palisaded villages of the Susquehannocks, against whom the Six Nations waged war for many years? It is known that the Tohocks, a tribe once residing at the head of the Chesapeake, did thus fortify themselves against the fierce Mingoes. How soon the past becomes mythical and legendary, and how greatly it is to be regretted that there has not been left more than mere conjecture of so much which, if known, would greatly interest us of the present!

> "Thus are the tracks of nations blotted out,
> Faint impress leaving, like the passing bird,
> Save when the mould, erst trod by them, is stirred
> By other races—giving to the light
> Some yellow, crumbling bone, or instrument of fight."

## THE MONUMENTS OF THE GIANTS.

When the French first settled Canada, they heard marvelous stories of a race of giants who were said to inhabit the country at the mouth of the Susquehanna and westward of that river. How much foundation of fact there was for these reports we do not know, but in after years the Susquehannocks were known as men of large size and of great strength. Six feet or more in height, and of corresponding weight, was the representation given of them by the first white explorers of their country. The knowledge of the Indians who first communicated to the French the stories of the size and strength of the Susquehannocks might have been traditionary and descriptive of a race who had been gigantic in stature and of herculean strength, but who, from some unexplained and unexplainable causes, had in the progress of time degenerated to the proportions of ordinary mortals. Students of ethnology know that such degenerations have occurred. There are some slightly presumptive proofs that the traditionary stories of the physical proportions of the original dwellers by the Rocks of Deer Creek are not without some slight basis of truth. The King and Queen Seats are the sitting places of giants, and they, presumptively, were occupied at a time past indefinitely distant by the rulers of the country. Indian Jupiters and Junos, honored not less, perhaps, than the gods and goddesses of Roman and Grecian mythology, may have received there the homage of their subjects. The gods have come down to us, said the superstitious

Ephesians, when Paul and Barnabas wrought miracles in their city. The gods are with us, would have been the natural exclamation of the superstitious Indians assembled in council on the summits of the Rocks in the presence of their rulers. We may not in this argument overlook the attractions but little noticed by intelligent seekers of curious objects which we have appropriately named, as we think, the Monuments of the Giants. On the summit of Rock Ridge, northeast of the Rocks, are several huge pillars of stone many feet in height. The curious observer that looks at them from the valley below in the dawn of the morning or twilight of the evening can scarce resist the conviction that they may have been erected by a race of giants in honor of their monarchs and to perpetuate their glory; and that here may have been deposited their remains, a use to which some, if not all, of the great mounds in the valleys of the Ohio and Mississippi were appropriated. The geologist who shall visit these attractions may smile at that simplicity which attributes to the might of man that which may be only a proof and illustration of the power of nature, which, in the indefinite past, threw upon the summit of Rock Ridge these collossal piles. But whatever was the agency by which the result was effected, there they are—those monuments

> "That look like frowning Titans in the dim
> And doubtful light,"

to be numbered with the many curious and attractive natural objects seen in the vicinity of the Rocks of Deer Creek.

The view from the Monuments is commanding

and extensive. In the distance northward is seen the Susquehanna River, and beyond it the hills of Lancaster County, Pennsylvania; southward, the Chesapeake Bay and the Eastern Shore of Maryland —the bay dotted here and there with white sails, moving gracefully, like swans, upon the bosom of the scarcely ruffled waters. On every side are reaches of fields and forests, in the midst of which are towns and villages, hamlets and farm-houses, constituting rare pictures of Arcadian beauty; the interest heightened by the lowing of the herds which feed upon the contiguous meadows, and by the sounds of distant church bells, reminding the devout of the hour of prayer, or summoning them to the worship of the sanctuary on the early Sabbath morning. The observer of these entrancing views is, however, conscious of that illusion which is always associated with such scenes; "every valley is an Eden, and every heart therein is at peace." The repose is the possession of unthinking nature; the hearts of the reasoning inhabitants are the abodes of strife, for in them is found envy, and pride, and ambition, and hate,

> "Every prospect pleases,
> And only man is vile."

## THE FIELD OF DARTS.

One-half mile southeast of Rock Ridge, and two and one-half miles northeast of the Rocks and bordering on the Mine Old Fields, is a valley in which have been found numerous Indian arrow-heads or darts. The stone of which they were made is unlike any that exists in that locality. Either the material of which these points were manufactured was brought there for that purpose, or it was the place of a great battle or battles fought by contending savage forces. Possibly, those confederated nations, Oneidas, Cayugas, Senecas, Mohawks, Onandagoes and Tuscaroras fought at that spot the Delawares and Susquehannocks, also confederated tribes, and that that contest was decisive of that long-continued struggle which reduced the latter nations to the condition of women, which they were contemptuously called after their subjection. No conjecture is at fault in considering that eventful past in which almost every foot of territory occupied by them was the place of battle between opposing Northmen and Southmen, and no excess of imagination can paint in too vivid colors the horrors of the struggle. To the Southmen the coming of the Northmen was as the coming of Gog and Magog. All resistance was vain. Loups and Susquehannocks were as helpless in the grasp of their foes, as effete Romans in the hands of Goths and Vandals.

History is ever repeating itself. Three centuries later the territory south, and bordering on the former, was the theatre of a contest between civilized people almost unparalleled, in its violence, in the history of warfare, resulting as in the past in the triumph of the warriors of the northern lakes and rivers, but as also in the past, without loss of honor to the conquered. The weaker was overborne by the stronger. Once more, if the prophet is indeed a seer, the mighty tribes of the distant North will move down upon the strong ones of the South. Russ and American in the valley of the Mississippi contending for the mastery, the former finding that valley the place of graves. So shall close the conflict of the world, and the earth shall keep jubilee a thousand years. The voice of Gitche Manito, the mighty, will yet be potent to subdue man's stubborn nature, and to allay his thirst for human blood. Happy would it be for mankind if his counsels were now heeded:

> "O, my children! my poor children!
> Listen to the words of wisdom,
> Listen to the words of warning
> From the lips of the Great Spirit,
> From the Master of life, who made you!
>
> "I am weary of your quarrels,
> Weary of your wars and bloodshed,
> Weary of your prayers for vengeance,
> Of your wranglings and disunion,
> All your strength is in your union,
> All your danger is in discord;
> Therefore be at peace henceforward,
> And as brothers live together."

## THE CHROME PITS.

Southwest of the Rocks, from one to three miles distant, are extensive deposits of chrome. They have been worked for many years, chiefly by the Messrs. Tyson, of Baltimore, enterprising merchants of that city. The working has often been intermitted for considerable spaces of time, but when the Baltimore and Delta Railroad shall have been completed, this industry will doubtless be continuous, and also enlarged, and thus add materially to the wealth of this section of the county of Harford. In addition to chrome, there are in the neighborhood valuable deposits of iron ore, magnesia, black lead, flint, asbestos and natural paint. The development of all these sources of material prosperity is but a question of time and of cheap transportation to market. The rock of Rock Ridge, which is fire-proof and particularly adapted for furnace hearths, may of itself become a considerable source of income. As an item of history interesting to all, it may be noted that the fire-proof character of these rocks was first discovered by Dr. Thomas Johnson, of the United States Army, and brother of the late Mrs. Eliza A. Preston, of Deer Creek.

## THE SLATE QUARRIES.

The Slate Quarries of Harford County, Maryland, and York County, Pennsylvania, are distant about eight miles northeast of the Rocks. They are a source of prosperity to the section of country in which they are situated, and promise, upon the completion of the Baltimore and Delta and York and Peach Bottom Railroads, to develop its wealth indefinitely. The slate is of superior quality, and held in high estimation wherever used. The quarries employ many men and afford subsistence to many families. The Welsh alone, who are chiefly employed, constitute a population of six or seven hundred. The village of Bangor, upon the summit of the Ridge, is composed principally of this nationality. It has several stores and other places of business. There are two churches, Welsh Congregational and Calvinistic Methodist. One of these has a settled pastor, the Rev. Mr. Hughes, and in both the Welsh language is exclusively used in religious services. These churches have given a desirable moral tone to the community, though, like all other Christian communities, the good find in the natural antagonism of the human heart a constant incentive to holy work. The village of Delta, at the foot of the Ridge, is composed chiefly of a native population. It has many places of business, but no church. In the immediate vicinity of the two villages are Slate Ridge, Slateville and Mt. Nebo churches, the first under the pastoral care of the Rev. Joseph D. Smith, a gentleman loved by his congregation, and held in high esteem by the people generally, irrespective of creed or profession; the second by the Rev. Mr. Davenport, a gentleman of deserved popularity among all classes; the last is under the charge of the Rev. Mr. Litsinger, of the Methodist Protestant Church, a Christian minister of enlarged and liberal views, whose praise is in all the churches.

The representative business men at the Quarries of the Welsh population are Faulk Jones, William E. Williams, John Humphreys and Hugh C. Roberts, Esqrs., John Parry & Co., Richard Reese & Co., Wm. C. Robertson & Co., John W. Jones & Co., Richard Hughes & Co., Robert L. Jones & Co., and Humphrey Lloyd, Esq. These gentlemen came to America in their youth, and by industry and skill have accumulated property; and occupying prominent and influential positions in the community, have given proof that industry and integrity are roads to success.

The first Welsh worker in the Quarries was a Mr. Davis; the first successful worker a Mr. Parry. The latter leased from Major Williamson thirty or thirty-five years ago, acquired a fortune, traveled into foreign countries, and died at Jerusalem. His family is now living in Bangor, Wales, on the interest of the money made at Bangor, United States of America. He is represented to have been a man of great integrity, a proof of which is, that after his return to Wales he called together his creditors, and paid the whole amount of his indebtedness to them, with interest.

The Quarries constitute a part of the group of interesting objects that render the locality of the Rocks of Deer Creek one of great attraction, and the visitor to the Rocks will do well to visit them. The Quarries have a promising future. Delta's magnificent distances will be of the past, and Bangor's sombre residences will be substituted by more pretentious edifices. The whole ridge will be alive with busy and enterprising workers, bringing from the bowels of the earth the material that shall shield its purchasers from sun, and rain, and snow, and make fortunes for the sellers.

## THE HORSE EPIDEMIC AND THE GUINEA-MAN'S PONY.

MORE than one hundred years ago, during the lifetime of Benjamin Rigdon, grandfather of the late George W. S. Rigdon, an epidemic among horses, very destructive in its character, prevailed throughout all this section of country. Tradition tells us that the Durhams, ancestors of the present families of that name, who were wealthy, owning large tracts of land and many horses, lost two hundred of them by the scourge; that the only horse that escaped the plague was a pony owned by an aged Guinea-man belonging to the first Mr. Rigdon. This old negro lived in a small cabin on the top of Rock Ridge, a short distance above the present residence of Richard Mayes, Esq., and not distant from the Rocks of Deer Creek. Whether the preservation of the life of the pony was owing to the healthfulness of the spot, or its isolated position, is not known; most likely to the latter, as the disease was, doubtless, contagious. Though not another representative of the equine race was left, the fortunate pony ate sprightlily of the slight herbage that grew on the open places of Rock Ridge summit, or of the corn grown by his thrifty master on the plain below. Looking down on the vast reaches of country on either side of the noted ridge, which towers in mountain height above the valleys, if he could not say, with Alexander Selkirk (Robinson Crusoe), on the island of Juan Fernandez,

> "I am monarch of all I survey,
> My right there is none to dispute,"

he could say, "I am the sole owner of a horse in all these broad domains;" and the proud pony, joining his master in the refrain, could utter,

> "No pent-up Utica contracts our powers,
> The whole boundless continent is ours."

Theirs it was not as against superior man, who rules the beasts of the field, but as against the beasts themselves, every one of which, save the pony, had succumbed to the power of the fell destroyer. The invulnerable pony was alone in all his glory. The value of such a pony could not be estimated.

The Guinea-man was a character. We write only of his religion. In that he was Fetish. He bore constantly about his person a *feitico*, the Portuguese name for an amulet—a talisman. To this *gru grus*, the name of the charm in his native language, he attached much importance, as it shielded

his family and all living things belonging to it—
dog or cat or *pony*—from disease, and made all safe
from the machinations of their enemies. We are
not to infer from his possession of the *feitico*, and
the power he ascribed to it, that he had no idea of
a Supreme Spirit, a King of Heaven, or that he did
not worship Him. Worship of the Highest is universal. So thought Pope:

> "Father of all in every age,
> In every clime adored,
> By saint, by savage, and by sage,
> Jehovah, Jove, or Lord."

The Guinea-man could not but recognize Him who

> "Warms in the sun, refreshes in the breeze,
> Glows in the stars, blossoms in the trees,
> Lives through all life, extends through all extent,
> Spreads undivided, operates unspent."

Fetishism is not a primitive religion. *It is a cor-
ruption of religion,* and even enlightened Christians
may well be fearful of the *feitico*, for the tendency
to idolatry is universal. Solomon built altars for
Chemosh and Moloch. The possession of the *feitico*
by the Guinea-man of Rock Ridge rendered him
very obnoxious to his fellow-servants. They were
afraid of him. "He possesses a charm," said they;
"he can kill us if he will. He is a wizard, a con-
jurer; his old woman is a witch; they deal with
spirits." No one of them would have touched that
mountain, for to touch it was death, they thought.
If they could have taken his life by poison, the usual
mode of their race, they would not have done so;
for does not the power of the *feitico* survive after its
possessor has gone hence, and may not his spirit

come in the silent hours of the night to avenge his wrongs? This apprehension was his castle. A cabin without wall, or moat, or drawbridge, was stronger than a feudal castle. It was defended by *superstition*.

That pony should have been skinned at its death, his cuticle stuffed and preserved, and labeled, "The sole survivor."

## THE CHURCH OF THE ROCKS.

"A city set on a hill" cannot be hid, nor can a church in such a position. This is eminently true of the house of worship now in the occupancy of the religious denomination known as the Evangelical Association. Situated on the summit of a lofty eminence directly opposite the Rocks, having them in full view, and overlooking the romantic and picturesque valley of La Grange, it looks upon a scene of alternate and mingled beauty and grandeur not often seen. This view has a peculiar psychological effect upon the intelligent and appreciative beholder. It intuitively demonstrates (I hope my language is philosophical) the former existence of a Rock Ridge Lake. That mighty basin, scooped out of the mighty hills which surround it, and the violent breaks of the Ridge, where the waters of Deer Creek rush through it, are physical proofs of its past existence, that, like axioms in mathematics, are self-evident.

Years previous to the building of the church, religious services were held on the summit of the Rocks. Prompted by curiosity, if by no worthier motive, there gathered once on that high eminence a congregation of men, women and children to hear the preacher of righteousness, who, we may well conjecture, was, with his audience, inspired by the scenes around them. In the selection of this spot for the exercise of his vocation, he but imitated the example of One greater than himself. "And seeing the multitudes, He went up into a mountain, and when He was set, His disciples came unto Him; and He opened His mouth and taught them."

More than a century previously there was a gathering of the chiefs of the Indians whose habitations were not distant from the Rocks, to listen to a sermon by a Swedish minister. The lessons were those which are now given to such as sit under the ministry of the Word. The clergyman spoke to them of the principal historical facts of Christianity—such as the fall of Adam by eating an apple, the coming of Christ to repair the evil, His labors, sufferings and miracles. When he had finished, one of the chiefs, thanking him for the discourse, related one of the mythical traditions of his people, which he deemed to be of like credibility, and equally binding upon the faith of all, and thus proved the inefficacy of the lessons taught him by the Christian teacher. Now, the lessons taught in the Church of the Rocks are doubtless believed, and, we would fain hope, practiced.

## MIKE'S ROCK.

A FEW miles northeast of the Rocks of Deer Creek, and on Rock Ridge, is a large rock known by the name of the title of this article. By the side of it is a large tree, the branches of which overhang it. An unfortunate, wearied with the perplexities of life, perhaps its agonies, closed here that life, if not precisely in the manner expressed in the following lines of an atheist, found among his papers after his death, yet in one of the modes common to the sad who lack fortitude:

> "An hour more;
> Sixty minutes, and the light
> Of this, we mis-call life, goes out forever.
> Forever? Aye; beyond the grave is found
> No life, save that great primal force, which here
> Displays itself alike in growth of weed
> Or human soul. Why longer live and suffer,
> *When the finger upon this slender*
> *Bar of steel will end, with one sharp flash,*
> *The hurry and the heart-ache?*
>
> ——"Death's messenger,
> From out this glittering tube, I call, to bid
> Me sleep; and in that sleep I dread no dreams,
> And no to-morrow. *Salve, rex terrorum!*
> *Moriturus te saluto.*"

A rash act, which was followed by a surprise. Death terminates this, not that; and that is eternal.

## THE ANCIENT MILL AND THE HONEST MILLER.

HALF-WAY between the Indian Cupboard, the retreat of Alexius, the noted fisherman and trapper, and the Otter Rock, above which was the habitation of Walter the Hermit, is an ancient mill. The first mill was of logs, and owned by an Englishman named Sankey. He was probably a Yorkshireman, as tradition informs us that the boys of that day amused themselves with his, to them, singular brogue. The mill, in the course of time, passed to Underwood, Harry, Morton, and J. Bond Preston, in the order named. This mill has furnished for many years bread for man and "stuff" for beast. One possessed of good descriptive powers and of a poetical genius might make the mill and its picturesque surroundings furnish material for an article that would not discount the reputation of *Scribner* or *Harper*, or any other leading magazine. Such description is not sought. Attention is directed to it rather because it is one of the ancient landmarks or watermarks of its neighborhood, and is a connecting link between the distant past and the immediate present. It derives also some notoriety from the snake story of the ancient trapper, a snake rivaling the sea serpent that has been so often seen on our Atlantic coast—from New England to Key West—the habitation of which was on the wooded hill opposite it.

In this ancient mill was once upon a time, as tradition tells us, an *honest* miller. To me, all millers are honest; but unhappily for the reputation of the craft, suspicious people, or people who, like the Heathen Chinee, as Bret Harte tells us, themselves familiar with the ways that are dark, are sometimes oblivious of the saying:

> "Who steals my purse steals trash,
> But he who filches from me my good name
> Takes that which does not himself enrich,
> And makes me poor indeed."

The honest miller was Thomas Wright, remembered by the few ancient people who have survived him. The story of the mysterious pig is both a proof and illustration of the integrity of the miller. Once on a time he left Sam's Creek, Carroll county, Md., early on the morning of a summer day, for the mill on Deer Creek. He had walked but a short distance when he heard the squealing of a diminutive pig that was following in his tracks. To escape the animal that was intent upon accompanying him on his journey, he left the road, walking through fields and forests. But in vain. The pig was equal to the emergency, its instincts pointing out the way of the miller unerringly. The integrity of the miller consisted in this, that he made every possible exertion to escape from that pig, showing that if there has ever been in this Christian country a miller who fattened his pigs on other people's corn, he was not that miller. The sad thing about the story of the pig is, that the honest miller, being of superstitious turn of mind, interpreted its singular following as an omen of his death. His death did occur a short time thereafter.

The wheels of the ancient mill yet turn—not the wheels used when the honest miller was occupant, but turbine wheels. The old mill is doomed. The coming narrow-gauge, insuring facility of transit to and from our large commercial city, will make it a potent reason why men of capital should utilize the great and continuous water-power for manufactories on a larger scale.

The unceasing flow of the waters of Deer Creek symbolizes the onward flow of humanity uninterrupted by successive generations. Humanity lives and the waters flow on, and such may be for a billion of years to come. But within the hearing of the music of no onflowing stream will there be, if my informant has uttered truth, a more honest miller than Thomas Wright. "An honest man is the noblest work of God."

"At the window, looking upon a crystal stream,
There sat a little lady, indulging in a dream,
A dream of fairy visions comes up before her eyes,
As she gazes now intently upon the azure skies.

"A soft breeze fans the valley, the sun rests on the hill,
The water murmurs sweetly as it rushes past 'the *mill;*'
The earth seems glad of springtime, unfolding every hour
From Nature's store, the tender bud that holds the fragrant flower.

"The lady sits a-dreaming, with head buried in her hand,
And visions come a-trooping from off a fairy-land,
And in her dreamy fancies there is a potent spell
That acts like charm of music, the smiling lips now tell.

"The heart cons o'er its treasures glowing in rosy light,
The spirit basks in beauty like stars that gem the night,
And thus the little lady dreamed happy hours away,
So happy in her musings she fain would have them stay."

The little lady whose musings form a proper sequel to the story of the ancient mill and its occupant, cherishes now, and it will ever be so, the highest admiration and esteem for the honest miller.

## THE OLDEST INHABITANT.

The oldest inhabitant now living in the vicinity of the Rocks of Deer Creek is Mrs. Rebecca Smith. She was born within three-fourths of a mile of her present residence. Here, within sight of the Rocks, she has lived to be almost a centenarian, being now in the ninety-sixth year of her age, surviving all who commenced with her the journey of life. Of a cheerful disposition and vigorous constitution, she has borne the burdens of life with comparative ease; and in a serene old age, comforted by loving hearts, she is awaiting resignedly the final summons.

Retaining unimpaired her mental faculties, which were always strong, she is able to entertain the curious of a later generation with most interesting descriptions of the habits, customs and manners of her early cotemporaries, distinctly recollecting and graphically relating innumerable incidents of the far past. In her youth this portion of the country was comparatively a wilderness. Without attractive and comfortable residences, as now; no convenient and well supervised roads, paths usually; no churches, preaching in private houses; the school-house a rude cabin of logs, without any floor but nature's, the chimney built of sticks, unplaned seats, without backs. Carriages there were none, the ordinary mode of travel being on horseback. The whole progress for ninety-six years, from the rude past to the present more advanced civilization, has been witnessed by her. But whatever contrasts she makes between the past and the present, they are without invidiousness. All along she has accepted the conditions of life, and the circumstances attending it, as they were more or less favorable, without murmur or complaint, recognizing the fact that the Most High appoints the bounds of our habitations, and that all things promote the happiness of the submissive.

It was her great felicity to be united in marriage, at a comparatively early age, with a gentleman of superior intellectual and social qualities, a conscientious Christian, a faithful friend, and a considerate and loving husband and father. The name of Amos Smith is to this day in this community a synonym of all that is excellent in character—it is as precious ointment poured forth. The memories of his unobtrusive acts of kindness are treasured, and his example valued as a rich legacy to those who have followed him.

The venerable matron, the oldest inhabitant of the neighborhood of the Rocks of Deer Creek, now leaning upon her staff, and bending toward that house of the earth that is the decreed abode of all, suggests, in the remarkable vigor of her physical being, and in the sprightliness of her intellectual life, lessons of wisdom that the young everywhere may with profit learn. An active life and a cheerful mind were the great treasures she possessed—

more valuable than gold or silver, or the jewels that blaze in the coronets of queens.

## THE YOUNGEST INHABITANTS.

The youngest inhabitant in the neighborhood of the Rocks is William Cecil Gladden, infant son of our well-known fellow-citizen, William Gladden, Esq.

Of the immediate vicinity of the Rocks, the youngest inhabitants are Bessie and Jessie, twin daughters of Joseph Wetherill, Esq., proprietor of the store at that place. Born under the very shadows of the Rocks, and by the side of Deer Creek, in view of the plunging waters of its romantic fall—all that remains of the once majestic cataract of Rock Ridge Lake—they are passing their confiding and unsuspecting life happy in the present and without care for the future. These children and William Cecil Gladden are cousins. May life be to the three all that fond parents and loving friends can wish. To each we dedicate the prayer of the gifted Willis:

> "Light to thy paths, bright creature! I would charm
> Thy being if I could, that it should be
> Ever as now thou dreamest, and flow on,
> Thus innocent and beautiful, to heaven."

## THE ORIGINAL INHABITANTS.

The original inhabitants were the Susquehannock Indians. Their territory extended from the Susquehanna River westward as far as the Allegany Mountains. This nation had a close alliance with the Len Lenapes or Delawares, who occupied the country from the head of the Chesapeake Bay to the Kittatinny Mountains northward, and as far eastward as the Connecticut River. This confederacy carried on a long war with the Indians who lived to the north of them, between the Kittatinny Mountains and Lake Ontario, who called themselves Mingoes, and were called by the English the Five Nations. At the time of the settlement of Jamestown, Virginia, this war was raging with great fury. In one of Captain Smith's excursions up the Chesapeake, at the mouth of the Susquehanna, in 1608, he met with five or six canoes full of warriors who were coming to attack their enemies in the rear. Having made peace with the Adirondacks, through the intercession of the French, who were then settling Canada, they turned their arms against the Lenapi and their confederates, and subduing them, reduced them to almost the condition of slaves. Peace was granted them on condition that they should put themselves under the protection of the Mingoes, confine themselves to raising corn, hunting for the subsistence of their families, and no longer have the power of making war. This is what the Indians call making them women. In this condition the Lenapes and their confederates were when the settlement of Pennsylvania was begun. What is said by Stith of the language and dress of the Susquehannocks, may deserve to be here inserted: "Their language and attire were very suitable to their stature and appearance; for their language sounded deep and solemn, and hollow, like a voice in a vault. Their attire was the skins of bears and wolves, so cut that the man's head went through the neck, and the ears of the bear were fastened on his shoulders, while the nose and teeth hung dangling upon his breast. Behind was another bear's face split, with a paw hanging at the nose. And their sleeves coming down to their elbows, were the necks of bears, with their arms going through the mouth and paws hanging to the nose. One of them had the head of a wolf hanging to a chain for a jewel, and his tobacco pipe was three-quarters of a yard long, carved with a bird, a deer and other devices at the great end. His arrows were three-quarters of a yard long, headed with splinters of a white, crystal-like stone in the form of a heart, an inch broad and an inch and a half long. These he carried at his back in a wolf's skin for a quiver, with his bow in one hand and a club in the other." Such was the appearance of the first inhabitants of Deer Creek and the Rocks. The Mingoes came, saw, conquered, and, occupying the country as masters, ruled for a time. They, in turn, were overborne by a superior race, and we have only the recollections of the deeds of the bold warriors.

## THE MASSACRE OF THE MINGOES.

The Mingoes of Deer Creek, as a body, left this locality in the year 1752. A few of them remained until, as is plausibly conjectured, the winter of 1763, and left immediately after the extermination of their kindred who had been living on Conestogoe Creek, Lancaster County, Pennsylvania. These Indians were the remains of a tribe long settled at that place, and thence called Conestogoes. Upon the arrival of the English in Pennsylvania this tribe sent messengers to welcome them, with presents of venison, corn and skins, and the whole tribe entered into a treaty of friendship with the first proprietary, William Penn—a treaty *which was to last as long as the sun should shine, or the waters run in the rivers.* This treaty was often renewed—the *chain brightened,* as the Conestogoes expressed it—from time to time. This tribe was ultimately reduced to twenty persons—seven men, five women and eight children, when by one of the most cowardly and dastardly acts on record in all the protracted and bloody contests with the Indians, this handful of peaceable people were murdered in cold blood by fifty-seven Conestogoe *gentlemen (?).* On Wednesday, the 14th day of December, 1763, these cavaliers, mounted on good horses, and armed with fire-locks, hangers and hatchets, entered Conestogoe Manor, and surrounding the defenceless village, fired upon, stabbed and hatcheted to death three men, two women and a boy. Shehaes, an old man who assisted at the second treaty held with them by Penn in 1701, was among the slain. All were scalped, and their huts burned. The remaining Mingoes, absent at the time of the massacre—they were out among their white neighbors selling baskets, brooms and bowls —were taken into protection by the humane magistrates of Lancaster, and secured from harm, as they thought, in the work-house of that town. Fifty of the chivalry, whose names are worthy to be inscribed on the temple of *dis*honor as high up as the summits of the Rocks of Deer Creek, suddenly appeared before that town on the 27th of December, invested the work-house, and by gradual approaches, doubtless, assaulted, captured and put to death all that were left of the Mingoes—men, women and children, fourteen in all. The remains of the murdered victims were dragged into the street and exposed to view. The fifty patriots of the Simon Girty stamp then mounted their horses, huzzaed in triumph, and rode off, congratulating themselves on their victory.

"Ah! where are the *soldiers* that fought here of yore,
The sod is upon them, they'll struggle no more,
The hatchet is fallen, the red man is low;
But near him reposes the arm of the foe.

"The bugle is silent; the war whoop is dead;
There is a murmur of waters and woods in their stead,
And the raven and owl chant a symphony drear
From the dark waving pines o'er the combatants' bier.

"Sleep, soldiers of *merit!* sleep gallants of yore!
The hatchet is fallen, the struggle is o'er,
While the fir-tree is green and the wind rolls a wave,
The tear-drop shall brighten the turf of the *brave?*"

The Mingoes of Deer Creek, hearing of the massacre of their people, and fearing that their lives would not be secure even among the humane white inhabitants of their neighborhood, left to join their people in the West or South. Their fears were groundless. We have never heard that gentlemen of Maryland ever deported themselves toward defenceless women and innocent children as those Bayard-like representatives of the men of England who wore the red rose.

The Mingoes occasionally visited their former homes, but that for a few years only. In 1764, a year after their removal, a party visited a locality in the neighborhood of New Park, York County, Pennsylvania, ten miles distant from the Rocks. There was a wigwam still standing at that date on the farm now owned by Duncan Brown, Esq., then possessed by his paternal grandfather. They were seen walking around it, and seemingly viewing it with a curious interest. To Deer Creek and the Rocks a final adieu came. The descendants of the former occupants know of these localities only as the homes of their ancestors—the places where the bear, the wolf and the beaver were many, and where the eagle built her nest upon the High Rocks, beneath which their chiefs sat by their council fires.

## ROCKS LITERATURE.

I am not perfectly satisfied with the designation I have given to the communications in prose and poetry which I have selected for this place in this book. Rocks Literature is not poetical; and the title is justified only by the fact that these contributions have been inspired by the sublimities and beauties of that wonder of nature, the Rocks of Deer Creek, with their romantic contiguities and surroundings. Could I have said "The Curiosties of Literature," the name given by Disraeli the elder to that confessedly most curious collection of literary gems which bears that title, I should assuredly be content, assuming, of course, that my collection would bear some proper relation in their literary qualities to that unique gathering of rare intellectualities. No other title could I use, because the literature I collect bears relation to but one thing—the Rocks of Deer Creek and their surroundings. And I am shut up to the necessity of using the material I have, material not created by myself, save one short essay, but by others, and for the quality of which I am in no degree responsible.

I am not to be understood, however, as disparaging the efforts of the writers in prose and in poetry whose contributions I shall insert in this book. I have no doubt that many of the readers of them will derive both pleasure and profit in their perusal.

I make these contributions a part of this volume, because they are a part of the history, so to speak, of the Rocks, and because they show that the Rocks are potent in inspiration.

The literature of the Rocks is abundant—sufficient, perhaps, to make a volume respectable in size. It is in accordance with my plan to limit my collection to a few selections. The first was written some years ago by a girl of tender years, and was, perhaps, her first effort in such writing.

## The Rocks of Deer Creek.

"Nature, in her delineations, ever delights in giving variety to the beauty and magnificence of her creations. Mountain, hill, valley and plain have each their enchantments, but the Rocks of Deer Creek, situated in the upper section of Harford County, present to the lover of natural scenery a combination of attractions that nature, in her munificence, seldom deigns to lavish on her fair domains. The Rocks are several hundred feet in height, extending to a point that projects in solemn grandeur over huge masses of rock that lie scattered at their base." Having described the beauty of the adjacent landscape, she continues: "But the Rocks, apart from the lovely landscape that spreads around us, are ever the scene that must enchant the gaze, and infuse into the heart of nature's votary a mingled feeling of admiration and awe." She concludes: "The image of the scene is impressed upon the soul, and in the secret chamber of our being often will we view over again the Rocks of Deer Creek."

The next selection is a poem, written by a young lady of Long Island, New York. We give only the stanzas which describe the "King and Queen Seats:"

> "In ages past, so runs a legend old,
> These rocks were the wild home of warriors bold;
> Here they in council met, and warfare planned,
> Talked o'er the mighty secrets of their dusky band;
> I fancy how the echoes have rung out,
> The noisy clamor of their war-cry shout.
> Long years have passed away, the red man's tread

No longer echoes there; the wild, fierce tribe is dead,
And nought remains but memories alone,
And two rough seats hewn from the solid stone.

"These were the lofty thrones of King and Queen,
Spread now with moss and trailing vines of green;
We rested in their depths, and pictured rare
Visions of Indian beauties, wild yet fair;
All still and silent now, only the breeze
Comes whispering soft sweet stories through the trees,
And echoes only waken to the words
Of untold beauty in the songs of birds,
Those clearest, bell-like tones that float and ring,
Pronounce the mocking bird the woodland king."

The following was written by a lady, a native of, and now resident in, Harford:

Rocks of Deer Creek, I, a pilgrim,
　Wander up thy mountain side,
And beneath thy lofty summits
　Watch the sparkling waters glide.

Here upon this pile of ages,
　Where the Red Man's flight was stayed,
I, in contemplation solemn,
　View the mighty work displayed.

Think of Him who, out of chaos,
　Called this great mysterious world,
With its mountains, vales and waters,
　Like a picture fair unfurl'd.

Piled this mighty, rocky structure,
　Like some castle, grim and gray,
Sublime—mysterious—wrote upon it,
　A monument without decay.

List! methinks I hear "the voices
　Of the hills" that round me lie,
For one grand and solemn anthem
　Seemeth filling earth and sky.

And self is lost—forgotten e'en—
　As I list the soft refrain;
Surely God, the builder of you,
　Reigns upon this height supreme.

Misty clouds are upward rising,
  Like pure incense, to the sky,
Peace-offerings from the waters
  On this rock-bound mountain high.

Surely in this solemn grandeur,
  On this temple most sublime,
More ancient than the pyramids
  Of old, in eastern clime,

Man must see and feel a power,
  Great—beyond our mortal ken;—
Rocks of Deer Creek, veil'd in mystery,
  You must ever more remain.

MARY WARNER ROSS.

*Sandy Hook*, 1879.

That which follows are the meditations of one who discovers, in the vicinity of the Rocks, a singular fern. He is evidently in a philosophical mood, and has been disturbed, it may be, by the rash speculations of some modern scientists so-called.

### A REMARKABLE FERN.

Strolling one day of the past autumn along Deer Creek, in the vicinity of the Rocks, I was attracted by a species of fern with which I was not familiar. Upon examining it minutely, I found, to my surprise, and I must confess to my gratification, written upon the stem and each leaf of the fern the word Biogenesis: life from life, and from nothing but life. And recollecting that Sir William Thompson, President of the British Association for the Advancement of Science, in an address to the Society, incidentally refers to the theory of Biogenesis and its opposite theory, Abiogenesis (spontaneous generation), I sought that address, and found the following statement therein:

"I am ready to adopt as an article of scientific faith, true through all space and through all time, that life proceeds from life, and from nothing but life." I am not aware that Sir William had ever seen a specimen of the singular Deer Creek fern, or ever heard of it; but one cannot fail to note the agreement between the teaching of the fern and that of the distinguished President of the British Association. Anxious to know what that other distinguished member of the same Association, Professor Huxley, might have to say upon Biogenesis and its antagonistic theory, Abiogenesis, I turned to an inaugural address delivered by him to the British Association, in which Professor Huxley concedes that "the evidence, direct and indirect, in favor of Biogenesis: life from life, and from nothing but life, *for all known forms of life*, must be admitted to be of great weight." This utterance of the great inductive philosopher gave me great pleasure, as it seems to confirm the suspicion that possibly the Creator of all things wrote upon my fern the word Biogenesis: life from life, and from nothing but life. My satisfaction with this declaration of the philosopher would have been complete, had he not to this just admission, as I thought it to be, added: "But though I cannot express this conviction of mine too strongly, I must carefully guard myself against the supposition that I intend to suggest that no such thing as Abiogenesis (spontaneous generation) has ever taken place in the past, or will take place in the future. If it were given me to look beyond the abyss of geologically recorded time to

the still more remote period when the earth was passing through physical and chemical conditions, which it can no more see again than a man can recall his infancy, *I should expect to be a witness of the evolution of living protoplasm from unliving matter.*"
I was now in a quandary. When doctors disagree, who shall decide? And what estimate can I have of the veracity of my fern? Singularly, the philosopher whose just quoted utterance had tended to overthrow my cherished theory of life, and brand as false the teaching of the fern, comes to my relief. The philosopher does not account for life without a *metaphysical* cause. Hear him: "I, individually, am no materialist, but, on the contrary, believe materialism to involve grave philosophical error." His materialism is only a trick of logic; his faith is that all life has a transcendental, metaphysical cause. He vindicates the truthfulness of my fern.

The question is, where did my fern get its life? Who wrote upon its stem and leaves Biogenesis? My fern was *sustained* by inorganic substances. From such substances it extracted the nutriment of its life by a chemistry peculiar to itself. But whence its life? It cannot be that life is a phenomenon, evolved from the forces of unliving matter. Science does not say so. Matter is a basis of life; in it life manifests itself, and nothing more. Life, like matter in which it dwells, was created, not evolved from unliving forces. The life of my fern came from abroad. Its cause was the only cause, ultimate, spontaneous will. The Author of all life gave it life, and wrote upon its leaves Biogenesis.

My fern is perishing. Is this not singular? Strange that the living forces which built it up should now, that its vitality is gone, tear down the structure which they, with so much pains, constructed. The vital principle in my fern did for a time hold in abeyance the physical forces, but this having departed, its enemies triumph. My fern is returning to unliving dust. Whether it, Phœnix-like, will arise from its ashes, I do not know. And if its unliving dust should become the basis of other life, whether it will be the life of another fern, I do not know. Of this I am confident, if it shall be the basis of another life, upon that creation, be it rose or magnolia or fern, will be written Biogenesis: life from life, and from nothing but life.

If any of my curious friends would see a specimen of the Deer Creek fern, they can do so by searching the hills between Preston's Mill and the Rocks of Deer Creek.

## The Old Mill.

Opposite Mingo Hill, on the waters of Deer Creek, a few miles above the Rocks, is a quaint old mill. Of this ancient mill a poetess writes:

> "Softly dim twilight lingers
>   O'er the picturesque mill,
> Night, with her purple fingers,
>   Is draping each noble hill
> With the shadows she loves to muster,
>   And waft in the twilight down,
> Faintly outlined with the lustre
>   Which streams from his starry crown.
> Beautiful shadows that fall so still
> And nestle down on the silent mill.
>
> "Silent, for now the throbbing
>   Heart of the mill's at rest,
> And only the breezes are sobbing
>   O'er the water's breast;

Its ripples' musical splashing
  Seem crowning a dreamy song,
As o'er the high dam dashing,
  They hurry so swiftly along.
Laughing waters that scorn to feel
The ponderous weight of the old mill wheel.

"We sit in the night's dark splendor
  And list to the whippoorwill,
Breathing in accents tender
  Its moan o'er the night-wrapped mill,
And watch how the shadows linger
  O'er the tree-topped hill on high,
Till each waving branch seems a finger
  Writing against the sky.
And the spirit of night has awakened
  The fairies that surely dwell,
In the quiet depths of the woodland
  In some fair little hidden dell;
For the fire-flies twinkle their lights afar
Till each fairy lamp seems a tiny star.

"Brightly the summer dawning
  Gleams o'er the quiet mill,
And scattered far by the morning
  The shadows lift from the hill;
And the sunbeam's golden splendor
  Pours o'er the dewy earth,
While the birdlings' voices tender
  Thrill with sweetest mirth.
A morning concert given us free
Echoing sweet the softest melody.

"How lightly the water dances,
  How sparkles its crystal breast,
As each arrow of sunlight glances
  In quivering, gay unrest,
And the dewy morning breathing
  Tenderly touching now,
Silvery hair enwreathing
  An aged though cheerful brow.
For many years that are gone and dead,
The mill has echoed his gentle tread.

"And long may it echo the paces
  Of the feet that are walking toward
The golden gates of the city
  Leading to home and God.
Respected friend, I will carry
  Sweet memories as I roam
Of the picturesque mill in the valley,
  And the sweetly embowered home.
With sad regrets my song will fill,
And a fond *farewell* to the dear old mill."

"JAMAICA, LONG ISLAND."

---

WHAT immediately follows are the prophetic declarations of the resident of "Shirley, near the Rocks," who may be indebted, in a measure, to the scenes amid which he dwells for the strength of his patriotic inspirations and impulses. The Highlands of Scotland, the mountains of Wales and Switzerland, have ever been inhabited by peoples of patriotic sentiments and practically devoted to liberty. The dwellers by the Rocks are not an exception. The Eagle, which is the symbol of their country's majesty, soars above the summits of their mountains. They watch its lofty flights with pride, and aspire to equal eminence in their sentiments and aspirations. The lowlands are generally the places of wealth, and luxury, and enervation, with which the sentiments of personal independence and individual liberty do not usually co-exist.

The prophecy is a portion of a Centennial Address, delivered by the author, July 4th, 1876, in Ward's Woods, not distant from, and in view of, the Rocks, and is a legacy to the young men who shall be living in 1976; bequeathed to them with the hope that they will cherish an ardent love of country, and maintain the principles of their fathers.

## A PROPHECY.

The retrospect we have made very naturally suggests the prospect. What shall the future of our country be? Who shall forecast its destiny? Have we, by the marvelous rapidity of our growth in the hundred years past, exhausted our energies, and brought upon ourselves premature old age, premonitory of speedy death? Or, are we as Hercules in his cradle, possessed of a vitality and force and fertility of resources that shall be manifested in achievements that will surpass all that has been seen in the past of our history, and surprised the world with their greatness. We are in the infancy of our greatness, the beginning of a progress such as has not hitherto been seen, and of which the most sanguine could not possibly have dreamed. Mankind is standing on the very threshold of a new life, on a boundary line, about to launch out into an unknown future. The past is gone, the old landmarks are swept away, and fresh armies of thoughts, opinions and knowledge are breaking in upon the world. The jungle has been cleared, space has been almost annihilated, and the human mind, free from embarrassments that have interrupted its progress, is entering upon a series of essays and conflicts that shall ultimate in achievements far surpassing those of the past, and that shall carry humanity upward to higher planes rapidly and majestically. It may be centuries before the new life shall be matured. In the very "lisping infancy" of the new life humanity may be, but the child is born, and there shall follow the vigor of manhood and the ripeness of age. A sagacious thinker and observer has said: "A mighty impulse has come over the world lately. A time of looking forward rather than back has set in. Great inventions of all kinds are altering the face of the earth, making the conditions of life different, and raising the hopes and fears of men. Great discoveries are bringing with them all the eager wildness, all the enthusiasm for good or evil, that such unsettlements must always bring. The vast ocean of knowledge has found its Columbuses, and hearts beat high with the daily hope of fresh wonders being unveiled by new voyagers." Where, we ask, has this impulse been felt stronger than on this continent and with us? Where so much of change, of adventure, of achievement? Where in all the earth so much of enthusiasm, of earnest purpose, of determination to do all that lies within the range of possibility? There are barriers that no human invention can overcome; conditions beyond the range of mortal power. But within those great barriers which God has fixed to human progress, an almost infinite advance is certain. There are men of folly, as was Canute the Great, when he sat by the sea-shore, and said to the advancing waters, "So far shalt thou come, and no farther," who in the impotency of their reason may prescribe bounds to human progress, but that progress, as did the oncoming waves, will mock their folly and weakness. This continent, this nation, shall participate in this general onward movement, and in a degree exceeding all. The genius of the American people, their inquisitiveness, their steadiness of purpose, their inflexibility of will, their inventive qualities, their love of change, their ambition to excel, all point to a destiny of unparalleled grandeur. Our lofty mountains, our wide extended plains, our majestic rivers, are symbolic of the might and majesty of our coming greatness. Here, upon the shores of the Atlantic, on the banks of the Mississippi and the Missouri, and by the side of the Pacific, in mountain place and valley, shall be a teeming multitude of men building up in their strength a material, intellectual, social, spiritual empire, before which all other empires shall pale as the glow-worm pales in the presence of the sun. It will be the onward movement of thought, and feeling, and faith, and work, widening and deepening, and increasing in strength, until mighty in its volume and resistless in its force, it shall bear upon its bosom, as the flood bears the oak, all the treasures of wisdom and knowledge. This is my thought—it may be the dream of an enthusiast.

In one hundred years the population of the United States of America may exceed that of China; the area of territory, if extended, may embrace the whole of North America, and our progress in all other respects be commensurate. Then it will be that those then living will look back upon the epoch of the first Centennial as we, who celebrate it to-day, look back upon its beginning—as a day of very small things, and, as we do, congratulate themselves and the country on the progress made, differing from us in this, that their felicitations will be greater—proportionate to their increased prosperity. The realization of this hope will depend essentially upon one thing—that we remain at peace among ourselves. This unity of the nation is the pledge of its perpetuity, and the assurance of its high destiny. Not, indeed, that unity which is enforced by strength of will and power of bayonet, but unity of sentiment and affection, that unity of mind and heart which has its most striking illustrations and exemplifications in the virtuous household, each member of which, recognizing the significancy of the relation, performs its obligations. The hope is that Christianity, in its onward march, will so leaven society with its restraining and conserving influences, that human passions will not simply be held in check, but will be consecrated to virtuous purposes, the human heart responding always and unerringly to truth, and the life to noble aim.

Our fathers sought to erect the superstructure of American government upon a substantial basis, intending that in this ark of national safety their descendants should be secure when the tempests gathered. The fabric of government which they erected was no temporary expedient, to serve the wants of a day; it was built, as the pyramids were built, to resist the wear of ages, and serve the necessities of generations. Washington, and Adams, and Jefferson, and Madison, and Monroe, and all the illustrious host of worthies who laid the foundations of American nationality, were men not only of wisdom, but of conscience also, having in view, not the mere gratification of personal ambition and the aggrandizement of self, but the welfare of the whole people and of generations of people. To establish this government our ancestors toiled, and sacrificed, and poured out their blood, not anticipating that Catalines would ever be found among their descendants, who would conspire against the liberties of the people, but hoping and believing that they to whom had been bequeathed the precious legacy of American freedom, would cherish it as vestal virgins and priests of Inca cherished their sacred fires. The gift has so far been generally appreciated, and the men of this generation are bearing upon their shoulders the ark which contains the sacred things placed therein by the fathers of the republic. They cherish it as the ark of the Lord was cherished in the house of Obed Edom.

It is not within the power of man to foretell the time when this nation, having performed its allotted part in the great drama of the world's life, shall follow the peoples that have preceded it, and pass in mournful procession to the graves of dead nationalities. The race that forms this nation has, as we have seen, been distinguished above all other races for its vitality and force, resisting thus far that strong tendency to decay that characterized the nations that preceded it. It may follow in the footsteps of the nations that have gone before; but if true to itself, if it fulfills the destiny which the Divine hand has marked out for it, then when its cycle shall have been completed and the record made up, future races will look back upon its period as the brightest in human history. And that record, the brightest spot in human history, may be the roll of a thousand years.

Yea, if the period of the existence of the great nations of antiquity was ten centuries, ten times ten centuries may be the cycle of American history, the time when its record shall be made up. The sentiment of patriotism existing in such intense force in the bosom of every true American would place no limit to his country's life. To-day, moved thereto by the enthusiasm kindled by our recollections of the past and our faith in the greatness of our country's future, we all with one accord exclaim, Our country; may she live forever!

My fellow-citizens, we congratulate ourselves that we have lived to celebrate the Centennial. In honoring this day we do justice to the memory of our fathers who bequeathed to us our heritage—to their intelligence, their virtue, their bravery, their fortitude, their spirit of self-sacrifice. They have gone to their graves, and the worthiest monuments that we can erect to perpetuate their memories are the appreciation of their virtues and the imitation of their examples.

Fellow-citizens, we shall not live to celebrate another Centennial. Ere the coming century of our national existence shall have closed we will have passed away—been gathered to our fathers; but we shall leave a heritage worthy to be preserved by our posterity, and by them transmitted to the generations following.

## MASON AND DIXON'S LINE.

A FEW miles north of the Rocks of Deer Creek, in latitude 39 degrees, 43 minutes, $26\frac{8}{10}$ seconds, is the boundary between the States of Pennsylvania and Maryland. This line was begun in December, 1763, and concluded in the end of the year 1767. Its whole length is 244 miles, not all of which was laid out by the scientific gentlemen after whom it is called. They were prevented by fears of hostile Indians from proceeding further than Sideling Hill, a distance of 116 miles from the place of beginning. At the termination of every fifth mile is planted a large stone, having on one side the coat of arms of William Penn, and on the other or southern side, the Escutcheon of Lord Baltimore, the proprietaries respectively of the provinces of Maryland and Pennsylvania. Every mile is a smaller stone with the letter P on one side and M on the other. All these stones were brought from England. This line was fixed after eighty years of constant discussion, and thus was lost to Maryland much fertile territory. It was not surveyed in the ordinary mode, but established by mathematical and astronomical calculation. A survey was had in 1844, and the original line was found to be substantially correct.

## A LITERARY CURIOSITY.

IN the year 1661, the Rev. John Eliot, "the Apostle to the Indians," translated the Virginian Bible into the language of the New England Indians. The following specimen exhibits the Lord's Prayer (Matt. vi: 9-13):

9. Yowutche yeu nuppenantamook: Nooshun kesukqut quttianatamunach knowesuonk.

10. Peaumooutch kukketassootamdonk, kuttenautamoouk nennach ohkeit neane kesukqut.

11. Nummeetsuonqash asekesukokish assamaiinean yeuyea kesuked.

12. Kah ahquontamaiinean nummatchseonqash, neane matcheneukgueagig nutahquontamounnanog.

13. Ahque sagkompagunaiinnean en qutchhuaonganit, webepohquohwussinean wutch matchitut. Newutche kutahtaun ketassootamoonk, kah menuhkesuonk, kah sohsumoonk micheme. Amen.

www.ingramcontent.com/pod-product-compliance
Lightning Source LLC
Chambersburg PA
CBHW020121170426
43199CB00009B/585